BUCKNELL REVIEW

The Philosophy
of
John William Miller

STATEMENT OF POLICY

   BUCKNELL REVIEW is a scholarly interdisciplinary journal. Each issue is devoted to a major theme or movement in the humanities or sciences, or to two or three closely related topics. The editors invite heterodox, orthodox, and speculative ideas and welcome manuscripts from any enterprising scholar in the humanities and sciences.

This journal is a member of the Conference of Editors of Learned Journals

BUCKNELL REVIEW
A Scholarly Journal of Letters, Arts, and Sciences

Editor
PAULINE FLETCHER

Associate Editor
DOROTHY L. BAUMWOLL

Assistant Editor
STEVEN W. STYERS

Editorial Board
PATRICK BRADY
WILLIAM E. CAIN
JAMES M. HEATH
STEVEN MAILLOUX
JOHN WHEATCROFT

Contributors should send manuscripts with a self-addressed stamped envelope to the Editors, Bucknell University, Lewisburg, Pennsylvania, 17837.

John William Miller in 1952

BUCKNELL REVIEW

THE PHILOSOPHY
OF
JOHN WILLIAM MILLER

Edited by
JOSEPH P. FELL

LEWISBURG
BUCKNELL UNIVERSITY PRESS
LONDON AND TORONTO: ASSOCIATED UNIVERSITY PRESSES

© 1990 by Associated University Presses, Inc.

Associated University Presses
440 Forsgate Drive
Cranbury, NJ 08512

Associated University Presses
25 Sicilian Avenue
London WC1A 2QH, England

Associated University Presses
P.O. Box 488, Port Credit
Mississauga, Ontario
Canada L5G 4M2

The paper used in this publication meets the requirements
of the American National Standard for Permanence of Paper
for Printed Library Materials Z39.48-1984.

Library of Congress Cataloging-in-Publication Data

The Philosophy of John William Miller / edited by Joseph P. Fell.
    p.   cm. — (Bucknell review ; v. 23, no. 1)
    Includes bibliographical references.
    ISBN 0-8387-5185-7 (alk. paper)
    1. Miller, John William. I. Fell, Joseph P. II. Series.
AP2.B887   vol. 34, no. 1 B945.M4764
051 s—dc20
[191]   89-43150
                                        CIP

(Volume XXXIV, Number 1)

PRINTED IN THE UNITED STATES OF AMERICA

This issue of *Bucknell Review* is dedicated, without his foreknowledge, to George P. Brockway, whose long and unselfish labors have made possible the dissemination of John William Miller's philosophy.

Contents

Recent Issues of BUCKNELL REVIEW

Notes on Contributors

GEORGE P. BROCKWAY writes regularly on "The Dismal Science" for *The New Leader* and is the author of *Economics: What Went Wrong and Why*. He was for many years CEO and editor of W. W. Norton & Company, Inc., and edited the published works of J. W. Miller. He holds a Litt.D. degree from Williams College.

VINCENT M. COLAPIETRO, an associate professor of philosophy at Fordham University, has written on Peirce, James, Dewey, and Marx. He is the author of *Peirce's Approach to the Self* (1989) and is working on a book designed to introduce John William Miller's philosophy to contemporary readers.

ROBERT S. CORRINGTON is assistant professor of philosophy at The Pennsylvania State University. He has published articles in American philosophy, semiotics, hermeneutics, and philosophy of religion and has coedited *Pragmatism Considers Phenomenology* and Justus Buchler's *Metaphysics of Natural Complexes,* 2nd ed. The author of *The Community of Interpreters,* he is past president of the Karl Jaspers Society of North America.

JAMES A. DIEFENBECK taught philosophy at Southern Illinois University at Carbondale until his recent retirement. He has published *A Celebration of Subjective Thought* and has completed the manuscript of a companion volume adapting these ideas for a theory directed to the control of the development of organisms.

ROBERT H. ELIAS, Goldwin Smith Professor Emeritus of English Literature and American Studies at Cornell University, has written a biography of Theodore Dreiser, articles on numerous American writers, and *"Entangling Alliances with None": An Essay on the Individual in the American Twenties,* an interdisciplinary study.

JOSEPH P. FELL is Presidential Professor and chair of the Department of Philosophy at Bucknell University. He is the author of *Emotion in the Thought of Sartre* and of *Heidegger and Sartre: An Essay on Being and Place.* He currently serves on the International Board of Advisors of the Center for Advanced Research in Phenomenology and on the Editorial Advisory Board of *Heidegger Studies.*

11

ROBERT E. GAHRINGER graduated from Williams College in 1947 and received his Ph.D. in philosophy from Harvard in 1953. He has published extensively in philosophical journals and has taught at Bowdoin, Kenyon, Hamilton, Emory, and Bryn Mawr. Since 1973 he has devoted his time to writing and music and lives in Deering, New Hampshire.

HENRY W. JOHNSTONE, JR. is professor emeritus of philosophy at The Pennsylvania State University. He earned his doctorate at Harvard, and taught at Williams College from 1948 to 1952. He has published on logic, the self, and the nature of philosophical argument. He edits *Philosophy and Rhetoric,* and is a coeditor of the *Journal of Speculative Philosophy.*

GARY STAHL is professor of philosophy at the University of Colorado. His current concerns are with interdisciplinary studies focused on issues of war and peace. His publications are mainly in ethics and metaphysics, and he is engaged in writing a book on the emergence of the self.

CUSHING STROUT is Ernest I. White Professor Emeritus of American Studies and Humane Letters at Cornell University. Among his books are *The Pragmatic Revolt in American History: Carl L. Becker and Charles A. Beard; The American Image of the Old World; The New Heavens and New Earth: Political Religion in America;* and *The Veracious Imagination: Essays on American History, Literature, and Biography.*

STEPHEN TYMAN is associate professor of philosophy at Southern Illinois University in Carbondale. He has published a number of papers in the fields of German idealism, phenomenology, and existentialism. He is currently writing a book on J. W. Miller and a book on phenomenology and deconstruction tentatively titled *The Ecstatic Conscience.*

Introduction

IT is unusual for an established journal to devote an entire issue to a figure not already widely known. The justification for doing so in the case of the American philosopher John William Miller must be that his thought has an originality and depth out of all proportion to its current scant recognition. The reasons for this discrepancy between the inherent interest of Miller's thought and its public acknowledgment are spelled out in the course of the essays comprising part 1 of this volume.

Since familiarity with Miller's philosophy has until quite recently been limited to his students and a handful of others, several of the essays attempt in one or another way to establish a context within which the particular aspects of his thought explored in the volume may be situated and found more intelligible than were they presented in isolation. Among the authors of the essays, seven were Miller's students at Williams College and another was for several years a colleague at Williams; in interpreting Miller's thought, these individuals draw upon their firsthand experience of Miller's courses and in some cases on extensive philosophical correspondence with him as well. All of the remaining, and much younger, authors have consulted the Miller manuscripts in the Williams College Archives and are recipients either of Miller Research Fellowships or of Miller Essay Prizes from Williams College. My sole regret about this volume is that it cannot include contributions from those associated with Miller who have passed on: his students Larry Hackstaff, Holmes Hartshorne, Walter Kaufmann, and Warner Wick; his colleague Lawrence Beals; and his long-term philosophical friend Alburey Castell, caricatured as "Augustine Castle" in B. F. Skinner's *Walden Two*.

The essays which follow are arranged under three heads. The two comprising part 1, "The Orientation," are intended to prepare the way for all the subsequent essays. I have placed my own contribution first because it can serve to orient the reader unfamiliar with Miller and his philosophy in two ways: by providing basic information about Miller's life and by broadly delineating the thought contained in the five volumes of his work published between 1978 and 1983. In the other essay in this section, Robert E. Gahringer characterizes the central preoccupation of Miller's thinking as a "philosophy of philosophy" and shows how the adequate interpretation of this way of thinking must primarily attend to what Miller called "the constitutional" rather than to particular doctrines and data. Taken together, these initial essays should provide a preliminary sense of an orientation Miller sometimes called "historical idealism"—an idealism that renounces the absolutism, or the ahistoric premises, of its predecessors.

The second and largest part of this volume, "Some Basic Features of Miller's Philosophy," serves to flesh out the general way of philosophizing introduced in the first section by exploring in some detail several of its most characteristic aspects. James A. Diefenbeck considers Miller's conception of the self or agent, showing how this self defines and knows itself only through the environment its acts disclose. Diefenbeck then critically considers whether Miller's espousal of the free act is compatible with the notion of objective necessity also present in his thought. Henry W. Johnstone, Jr. explores another aspect of Miller's interpretation of necessity: the sort of "fatal" necessity Miller found in the historical transitions from one type of philosophy to another as Miller, in his influential introductory philosophy course, analyzed the way philosophy revises itself. Vincent M. Colapietro's essay takes up the central, and interdependent, Millerian concepts of midworld, symbol, functioning object, and utterance. This essay thus explicates in considerable detail what might be called the core of Miller's philosophy: the historical act as disclosing an environment and having to abide by the environment so disclosed.

Likewise concerned with Miller's interpretation of the interrelation of act and environment, Robert S. Corrington seeks to show how Miller's "finite idealism" sets his understanding of natural order apart both from absolute idealism and from the contemporary naturalism of Justus Buchler. The moral aspect of human agency is examined in the two essays which round out this section of the volume, both of which consider Miller's relation to Kant's ethical philosophy. Stephen Tyman analyzes how Miller revises Kant's account of the relation of freedom and desire in the individual, and how Miller's conception of the self-maintaining act resolves the "problem of evil" which plagues Kant's dualistic account of human willing. Tyman's concluding call for consideration of the convergence of the specifically historical and social aspects of Miller's ethics is answered by Gary Stahl's paper. Stressing Miller's rejection of all appeals to ahistoric criteria for making value judgments, Stahl shows how Miller's notions of historical act and midworld commit him to a social and institutional process in which alone values can be declared, maintained, and responsibility revised.

Part 3, "Relating the Philosophy to Other Disciplines," consists of essays written not by professional philosophers but by thinkers concerned with exhibiting some of the implications of Miller's philosophy for the fields in which they have written. Drawing extensively on his long correspondence with Miller, George P. Brockway shows how Miller's notions of the self-maintaining act and the functioning object can be fruitfully applied to the field of economics, thus generating an account of economic activity critical of prevailing conceptions of that process based on moral, physical, or psychological models. Again drawing upon correspondence—some of which offers glimpses of Miller's approach to aesthetics—Robert H. Elias demonstrates how Miller's conception of the purposive, revisionary, and environment-defining act can be employed to interpret the development of American history and literature. In the concluding essay Cushing Strout, tracing Miller's role in his own intellectual development, finds in Miller's philosophy an original synthesis of historicism and existentialism that makes possible the writing of nonreductive historical narratives. In these last three essays our attention is directed not only to the philosophy but to the man who advanced it in the medium of an extraordinarily rich philosophical correspondence with his former students as well as in more formal writings.

Thanks to the efforts of Henry Johnstone, it has been possible to include a bibliography of works by and about Miller which includes a description of the Miller section of the Williams College Archives.

For advice at several stages in the preparation of this volume I should like to thank George P. Brockway, Henry W. Johnstone, Jr., and Cynthia R. Fell. For research on a number of aspects of Miller's life and writings I am indebted to Sylvia B. Kennick, Archivist of Williams College, Sarah A. Polirer, Curatorial Assistant at the Harvard University Archives, and Rohit Sanghi, Graduate Research Assistant at Bucknell University. Katherine Miller has my profound gratitude for invaluable personal recollections. The editorial expertise of Dorothy Baumwoll has spared the reader many an inconsistency and infelicity.

JOSEPH P. FELL

BUCKNELL REVIEW

The Philosophy
of
John William Miller

I
The Orientation

Miller: The Man and His Philosophy

Joseph P. Fell

Bucknell University

THE American philosopher John William Miller was born in Rochester, New York on 8 January 1895. After attending public schools in Rochester, he studied at Harvard College in 1912–13. For financial reasons he transferred to the University of Rochester for the years 1913 to 1915, then returned to Harvard for his senior year, receiving his A.B. degree in 1916. After working for a year in a Rochester electric company he volunteered for ambulance corps duty in France with Base Hospital 44. In 1919, motivated to enter the field of philosophy by his experience of the First World War, he returned to Harvard as a graduate student in philosophy, receiving his master's degree in 1921 and his doctorate in 1922. Among his teachers were R. B. Perry and E. B. Holt, both of the realist persuasion, and W. E. Hocking and C. I. Lewis on the more idealist side; it was in the tension between these philosophical camps that Miller worked out his own stand.[1]

From 1922 to 1924 Miller taught at Connecticut College, during which time he married Katherine S. Gisel. In 1924 he moved to Williams College where, apart from interludes of summer teaching at the University of Rochester and Boston University and serving as acting professor of philosophy at the University of Minnesota in 1938–39, he spent the balance of his teaching career. The Millers' son Eugene was born in 1925 and became editor of a Connecticut newspaper; their second son, Paul, born in 1928, became a professor of philosophy at the University of Colorado. Miller chaired the Williams philosophy department from 1931 to 1955. From 1945 he was Mark Hopkins Professor of Intellectual and Moral Philosophy, an august title inherited from his predecessor and colleague James Bissett Pratt. He retired in 1960, characteristically refusing to be celebrated, and died on 25 December 1978 after a quiet but philosophically active retirement.[2]

For all of Miller's thirty-five years at Williams he was one of the greatest of American teachers. Yet, apart from the dedication of a number of books to him by former students, his profound influence on generations of students went largely unrecorded until

21

1980 when George P. Brockway published a vivid and accurate account of Miller's teaching in *The American Scholar*.[3]

Miller's career was amply justified by his classroom teaching. Prior to the last year of his long life, he had published only four papers/articles, and no one who benefited from his instruction thought that more was necessary. It seemed an evident case of a man whose wholehearted devotion to teaching had precluded reams of publication. Yet over the years he had in fact written a substantial number of essays which he apparently never submitted for publication, and he had conducted an elaborate philosophical correspondence. Toward the close of Miller's life, Brockway persuaded him to release this material for publication, and the initial volume, *The Paradox of Cause*, appeared in 1978, only months before Miller's death. The second volume, *The Definition of the Thing*, consisting of Miller's 1922 Harvard dissertation plus some later notes on language, appeared in 1980, to be followed by *The Philosophy of History* (1981), *The Midworld of Symbols and Functioning Objects* (1982), and *In Defense of the Psychological* (1983). Brockway served as editor of all five volumes, in some cases able to work from indications left by Miller for ordering the essays, in some cases faced by the sort of difficult organizational decisions that confronted the editors of the papers of C. S. Peirce.

The result is a most intelligently organized thematic selection comprising a complementary set of variations on a single theme that occupied Miller from first to last: the epistemological and ontological unity of persons and things. However, it is neither a critical nor a complete edition. For dates of the essays, and so a sense of the chronological development of Miller's thinking, the scholar must for the time being consult Miller's manuscripts in the Williams College Library.[4]

Why had Miller withheld the bulk of his work from publication? The self-imposed demands of his teaching seem to have been only part of the reason. Another was his "dated" style of writing; his essays were fashioned in a deceptively simple, almost colloquial, prose—sometimes reminiscent of Lincoln's and Emerson's though far harder to understand. But the primary reason was that Miller knew his thinking to be as unfashionable as his prose. At a time when others had abandoned philosophical idealism, he sought to revise it. He stuck to his guns as wave after wave of anti- or postidealist positions swept the American philosophical scene: critical realism, behaviorism, instrumentalism, logical positivism, linguistic analysis, existentialism. Characteristically, he found reasons for taking all of these stances seriously, yet in the last analysis he found most of them "ahistorical" in orientation, and he found none of them capable of coordinating the human and the natural in a manner that did justice to both. On these points he was insistent.

Miller will say, at certain critical junctures, "I don't like" such-and-such an idea.[5] This isn't an intrusion of arbitrary preference into his argument. It is rather a recognition that arguments are made by persons who are themselves at stake in their arguments, and Miller displays an uncanny ability to isolate the often-unspoken personal premises behind the arguments of a number of philosophers and psychologists. He was thoroughly impatient with that misallocation of philosophical energies which consists in analysis of particular arguments at the expense of attention to the personal "utterances" or basic takings of a stand that are "constitutive," that really control the use made of the arguments. He frequently reminds the reader that the objective or natural, an impersonal order, is revealed in consequence of a human will or demand or it doesn't turn up at all. The "paradox of cause"[6] is that in a world which comprised only natural causation, natural causation could not be disclosed. Subjective purposes and objective nature are mutually implicative, or their relation is "dialectical." To attempt to understand the personal entirely in terms of the impersonal is to rule out of court the very will and understanding that demand a stable and independent environment, thus launching the idea of an impersonal order in the first place. Those, such as B. F. Skinner, who wish to have an ordered environment but discredit free human agency, fail to recognize their own inevitable role in disclosing that environment.[7]

Miller characteristically reaches his own conclusions about the interrelation of man and nature by means of probing examinations—both sympathetic and critical—of the major interpretations of the self-world relation that have been generated in the history of philosophy. He sees each of them as an essay in "control"—a proposal of a general order (an "infinity" or "form") in terms of which man has tried to disclose the nature and interrelation of the particulars ("content") of his world. It is only by this will to control (to know, to utilize) his environment that man is able to gain real control (self-knowledge and personal efficacy) over himself. Thus, spiritualist and voluntarist philosophies arise out of the demand for a world in which purposes count (can be regarded as "ontological" or "constitutional"). Naturalisms arise out of the need for an environment independent of all purposes, one of ascertainable causes and predictable effects. Subjectivist and objectivist philosophies each arise from a demand that must be met, yet each destroys the other if it takes itself to be the whole story. The recognition that one needs *both* "purpose-control" *and* "cause-control" is the strong suit of the philosophy of dualism, which refuses to sacrifice cause to purpose or purpose to cause. But dualism fails in its inability to show how an originative human will and a natural order can coexist or interact. Postdualistic (post-Cartesian) positions such as empiricism, idealism, and pragmatism are shown to be efforts to interrelate the order of purpose and the order of natural causation.[8]

Thus far, Miller's tracing of the development of types of philosophy is reminiscent of, and frankly indebted to, the thought of Hegel and of Miller's teacher William Ernest Hocking. The history of philosophy exhibits philosophy's revision of itself by a dialectical development in which each successive type of philosophy satisfies a demand hitherto unmet, yet remains only part of the story of the human will to order itself and its world insofar as it takes its own particular story as the final or self-sufficient one. Philosophical revision thus has the form of a process of both persistence and change, in which the legitimate demand of each major[9] philosophy is inherited and preserved, while the claim of each philosophy to be the whole story is canceled.

Although Miller's philosophy, essentially a philosophy of history, is in these respects indebted to Hegel, he cannot accept Hegel's claim that this odyssey of self-revision culminates in "the absolute"—a final knowledge in which the human being has risen to the standpoint of God. Fond of Lincoln's assertion that "we cannot escape history," Miller remains humanistic and skeptical of all claims to theological finality. He was, he often said, wary of "mountaintop experiences." His temper is Kantian, with some affinity to American pragmatism, in that he argues that knowledge does not depend on completeness and absolute certainty. Insist in advance that truth be final and incorrigible and you doom yourself to skepticism. Philosophy must come to terms with finitude, contingency, the accidental. He wanted, he said, to "affirm the moment," to "give ontological status to finitude."

But how to do this? While Miller apprentices himself to the history of philosophy and finds it far more than a record of naive errors, he is an original thinker. He refuses, in fact, to see apprenticeship and originality as anything but complementary—another sign of the dialectical cast of his thinking. Responsible and relevant originality lies in "revising" an inheritance, and Miller sees a moral urgency in this. He maintains that the sole possible locus of defensible order and lawfulness is human history, but finds many of his contemporaries guilty of discounting it, suspicious of the precarious, all-too-human sort of order that history exhibits. His response: if you want an order that owes nothing to the human being, you'll end up with no real order at all. The quest for the safety and security of an ahistoric finality overlooks our own collective responsibility for maintaining an ordered environment. "If we want reverence, anything sacred and so imperative, we must advance now to history. . . . There is the common world, the actual one."[10]

History is precisely the region of human originality, of those human *res gestae* or "utterances" that "declare a world." No extra-historical or extraphilosophical conditions can account for these originative (or "unenvironed") utterances, for it is these utterances *themselves* that first propose or "project" the formal orders (e.g., mathematics, logic, causation) which are the prerequisites for finding causal conditions. Without this human history, no natural history; without this philosophical projection of the formal conditions necessary for knowledge (e.g., identity, difference, antecedent and consequent, etc.), no sciences. Such acts of will or utterances propose the controlling "norms" or "rules" presupposed by any particular disclosures. Anything that presents itself as real, fact, or datum can do so only within a formal order which determines what is to count as real, fact, or datum. In arguing for such free and "constitutive" formal ordering, Miller clearly sides with one particular part of his inheritance, philosophical idealism.

The genuinely basic and formative historical crises, whether in science or in society, are philosophical—not conflicts in detail but those in which one conception of the order of the whole is pitted against another. Here originality comes into play. Such constitutional crises are "the loci of radical disagreement." Philosophy is the history of these conflicts, a fate which thought must undergo once it has committed itself to the search for intelligibility and lawfulness and to the responsibility for its utterances and their consequences.

Hence the central problem posed by Miller's philosophy, and by post-Kantian thinking in general: if human proposals of an ideal order are prerequisite for the disclosure of real particulars, and if such proposals conflict with each other and none has any ahistoric or absolute guarantee, then must we not conclude that these proposals are simply competing human fictions? Miller allows that this is the historical juncture we seem to have reached, but holds that "The chaos of today [nihilism and skeptical relativism] is the historical consequence of a metaphysical lapse. . . . a consequence of the account of the world that the learned propagate. For them the actual has no authority and rates no reverence because it is not recognized."[11] Miller's bold and original crusade is for "the as yet unacknowledged actuality of the midworld."[12]

Miller rightly regards his treatment of "the midworld" as his primary accomplishment (though he finds it prefigured in Hegel and in Royce) and hence the 1982 volume of essays devoted to this topic is the apex of the series. The notion of the midworld, or region of the actual, challenges at its roots the inherently dualistic presumption that the sphere of human formal utterances is simply a sphere of "subjective" fictions or simplifications which has nothing in common with the region of natural reality from which these utterances allegedly cut us off. As Miller's most original notion, the midworld was met with incomprehension by most of his contemporaries. In an important letter of 1974 he wrote:

> My metaphysic requires what I have called "The Mid-World," i.e. the Actual. It is a statement that has brought me puzzlement and rejection.
>
> So, I am neither Realist nor Idealist. Locally it was held that since I was no Realist I must be an Idealist of the "Subjective" or the "Objective" sort. At the University [Harvard] it was assumed, or argued, that not to be a Realist was to be an Idealist. You had to be one or the other.

What is instead required, Miller goes on to say, is a "middle ground which could account for the genesis of the different."[13] This middle, the actual, has at once real and ideal characteristics that are abstractable from it. If Miller, as he did, sometimes consented to the labeling of his thought as an idealism, it was only with a qualifying adjective: "historical idealism," or, as in his Harvard dissertation, "a naturalistic idealism."[14] Any adequate interpretation of Miller's philosophy must, to grasp his originality, understand how and why these qualifying adjectives rule out any simple assimilation of his thought to traditional philosophical idealisms.

I shall not succeed here in doing justice to the idea of the midworld; the interested reader will want to consult at very least the entirety of the 1982 volume, and preferably the many implicit and explicit references to the notion occurring throughout the remaining Norton volumes as well. The importance of the notion for Miller is reflected in the frequency of its occurrence in the essays of the present volume. For a start, it is important to recognize that Miller doesn't pull the notion of the midworld out of thin air; he finds it illustrated again and again in the history of science and technology as well as in ordinary experience. Thus the mid-world is already present. The task is to recognize it and so take it into account philosophically. That it is difficult to recognize, and that philosophical talk about it sounds so strange, is owing to an "intellectualism" that has strayed from the nature of human action and its objects, chiefly because it has been felt that if you wanted an ordered world you had best keep the potentially unruly human element out of it. It has not been well understood that the conditions that permit disorder and error are the very same conditions that make possible avoidance of error and genuine knowledge of the real.

The midworld is to be seen as an historical process, to be identified by an analysis that goes back from the subjective and the objective, the ideal and the real, to their common genesis in concrete human activities of grappling with nature: "a genetically [historically] produced end [such as a science of nature] must not scorn the base degrees by which it has risen."[15] Miller warns the reader that his account of the origin and justification of the categories on which knowledge depends will be thoroughly "earthy." Either these categories originate in common human action and also find their justification there, or else they will be alleged to have a "transcendental" origin (as in Plato or Kant) that renders their application to the here-and-now experience of nature problematic—a kind of imposition from above. In other words: if thought and reality are not intrinsically conjoined from the beginning, there is no possibility of ending up with a thought that truly discloses reality. *Formal thought and reality emerge together, in the act.* The only possible basis, or orientating point, for any philosophical analysis is human action in history. (It would thus not be amiss to call Miller's position a Philosophy of the Act, or of Actuality.)

Miller defines the human act broadly so that it is coextensive with what he calls "utterance." In so doing, he intends to recognize that distinctively human action not only sees and uses but names (gives form or identity to) what it uses. Language is not a kit of tools which one might or might not use, but is rather the proposal of an order that organizes things as things in the first place.[16] No language, no intelligible world. In saying that this act of uttering is "original" Miller is claiming that it neither precedes nor follows the disclosure of things, contrary to most of the usual accounts of the relation of language, and action, to things. Absolute idealism or rationalism, holding that thought generates universal categories independently of experience, is wrong. Absolute empiricism, holding that experience of data occurs independently of thought, is equally wrong. The act or utterance, then, is the *simultaneous* disclosure of form and content, of universal and particular, of idea and datum.

For this to make much sense or have any plausibility, examples are needed. Miller generously supplies them. Many of them are drawn from mathematics—but not from "pure mathematics," for Miller holds that mathematics begins as, and has its final justification in, the disclosure of things. These examples are thus concrete illustrations of a primary Millerian thesis: that the pure/applied and form/content distinctions are derivative or abstractive ones. Utterances, including the utterances of mathematics and logic, are in their origins *at once* pure and applied. Form (universality, the systematic) occurs *in* an action that discloses content (particularity, the contingent). Example: he who so much as counts his toes has disclosed both the number of toes he has (a particular content) and the order of mathematics (an ideal or formal order). Another example (a favorite of Miller's): the creation of a yardstick not only to measure the distance between two points but to disclose objective space. Thereby the real puts in an appearance ("these trees five yards apart") and an ideal order is warranted (a system of mensuration).

Miller asks us to attend closely to the "ontological status" of the yardstick as a typical example of the actual. One cannot choose between regarding it as ideal and regarding it as real, subjective or objective, psychological or physical, human or natural, form or content, universal or particular, mathematical or material. No traditional "dyadic" account of it can tell us what it is; it challenges our usual habits of thought. It is, in Miller's terms, "triadic" or "actual." What is still missing in Kant is the story of the genesis of forms and categories in the actual, in historical utterances, and it is here alone that their validation can be found. The "actual" is, as the term would indicate, the correlate of an act—in this case, the act of mathematical utterance. *What is ontologically primary is actuality.* The actual is neither a mere personal function nor a mere impersonal object; it is a "functioning object" or "embodied utterance" or "incarnate word" or "unit of account," of which one important type is the artifact. While it is the embodiment of a human will to order, it is at the same time a "critic" of the merely subjective: the tree I thought to be fifty yards from my house turns out to be seventy-five. The act not only launches purposes but controls them. The world of words, numbers, time and space, of volts, atoms, and miles, of microscopes, telescopes, and clocks, is a midworld. The primary functioning object is the human body.

The crucial point is that the actual isn't an adding of the ideal to the real, or of thought to matter, as if we had prior separate experiences of the ideal and the real and, somehow, subsequently brought them into relation with each other. Miller's claim, on which his entire position stands or falls, is that both the ideal and the real appear thanks to the actual. "Both assured form and assured content derive from actuality."[17] In an important sense this isn't idealism—as opposed to realism or to naturalism—at all. It is a way beyond the idealist-realist controversy. The ideal and the real are mediated in the functioning object.

Through a complex series of arguments, Miller is able to show how the functioning object or actuality enables us to generate, to distinguish between, and properly to interrelate, appearance and reality, error and fact, contingency and formal order, purpose and cause, mind and body, even the humanities and the sciences. These arguments comprise the most adequate resolution known to me of the still-vexing problems posed by Cartesian dualism. If it is at all true, as is often claimed, that the philosophical dilemmas of the last three centuries are primarily the consequence of Cartesian formulations, Miller's concept of the midworld of functioning objects deserves an important place in the history of modern philosophy. One index of a fruitful philosophical concept lies in its enabling us to see a whole range of other notions in a new light, and in the course of Miller's writings such light is shed on many problematic notions, such as stimulus and response, freedom, fate, the moral, democracy, law, the accidental, sign and symbol, myth, quality, organism, intersubjectivity.

I do not know whether Miller's philosophy will gain the place due it, or whether it will receive only limited notice and then be forgotten. The latter eventuality would be tragedy. For those steeped in the problems of the post-Kantian philosophical situation and faced by the specter of nihilism—which may be all of us—Miller offers a response that is original and positive while neither idiosyncratic nor uncritical. In my judgment, we find in Miller's thought a compelling answer to the question of what remains of philosophical idealism once it is freed of its rationalistic excesses, its claims to ahistoric absoluteness—excessive claims that still haunt Edmund Husserl's transcendental idealism. After Miller, it is necessary to say that Marx, Nietzsche, and the existentialists have only tempered the claims of idealism, not destroyed them. Miller has demonstrated the original and ineliminable role of freely proposed categories in the constitution of human experience, but as *actual* conditions of objectivity rather than as subjective, idiosyncratic, or fictive bars to knowledge. The manner in which Miller has reconciled the claims of mind and its ideality with the claims of nature and its reality makes him one of the more provocative successors of Kant and Hegel. If his way of talking takes some getting used to, what he says is thoroughly contemporary. If he rejects all metaphysical claims of transcending history and its contingency, he nonetheless shows genuine science to be possible. I know of no saner *via media* between skeptical relativism and metaphysical certitude.

Notes

An earlier version of most of this paper appeared under the title "An American Original" in *The American Scholar* 53 (Winter 1983–84): 123–30.

1. Miller's dissertation committee consisted of Hocking, Lewis, and H. M. Sheffer. Among Miller's other teachers were Raphael Demos and L. T. Troland. For analysis of the positions taken by Lewis, Hocking, Holt, and Perry on the idealism/realism issue, see Joseph L. Blau, *Men and Movements in American Philosophy* (Englewood Cliffs, N.J.: Prentice-Hall, 1952), pp. 196–99, 276–93.

2. Some of the foregoing biographical data comes from the 25th Anniversary Report (1941) of the Harvard Class of 1916. I am indebted to Robert Corrington for calling my attention to this report. For further information I am grateful to Katherine Miller.

3. George P. Brockway, "John William Miller," *The American Scholar* 49 (1980): 236–40. Reprinted in Joseph Epstein, ed., *Masters: Portraits of Great Teachers* (New York: Basic Books, 1981), pp. 155–64.

4. See the last section of Henry Johnstone's bibliography at the end of this volume. It is likely that a complete listing of the dates and sources of all of the essays in the five Norton volumes will be published in the foreseeable future, together with a comprehensive index to these volumes.

5. E.g., J. W. Miller, *In Defense of the Psychological* (New York: Norton, 1983), p. 127.

6. See J. W. Miller, *The Paradox of Cause and Other Essays* (New York: Norton, 1978), pp. 11–18.

7. Miller's critique of Skinner can be found in *Defense of the Psychological*, passim.

8. I am here drawing, in part, on Miller's lectures in his introductory course, "Types of Philosophy," as given in the academic year 1950–51. This course forms the main subject of Henry Johnstone's paper, below. Robert Gahringer's extensive (106 pages) notes on the first semester (Philosophy 1) of this course as delivered in 1947–48 can be found in Box 22, Folder 13 of the Miller Archives. Some of Miller's own notes for the course can be found in Box 10, Folder 3; Box 15, Folders 3–4; and Box 17, Folder 22.

9. Where "major" means that it responds to a significant, defensible, or unavoidable human "demand" (e.g., for an ordered and intelligible environment; for the recognition of originative personal thought and agency), including the demand that an inherited philosophy be purged of defects incurred in its attempt to meet some demand.

10. Miller, *Defense of the Psychological*, p. 151.

11. Ibid., p. 105.

12. Ibid.

13. Letter of October 1974 to R. E. Gahringer, p. 1. In Miller Archives, Box 22, Folder 14.

14. J. W. Miller, *The Definition of the Thing* (New York: Norton, 1980), p. 149.

15. J. W. Miller, *The Midworld of Symbols and Functioning Objects* (New York: Norton, 1982), p. 8.

16. The claim that language is a tool is also effectively criticized by Justus Buchler. See his *Nature and Judgment* (New York: Columbia University Press, 1955), pp. 41–49.

17. Miller, *Midworld,* p. 178.

On Interpreting J. W. Miller

Robert E. Gahringer

I N his lifetime, John William Miller published only two short
essays in philosophical journals, one in a student literary maga-
zine, and one as an afterword to a translation of Ortega y Gasset.
This was not for lack of opportunity. Nor was it from a lack of
material. He did, however, write many letters to editors of news-
papers, notably the *New York Times* and the *Berkshire Eagle,* but
only a few of these were published. He consented to the publication of his essays only as he approached death, and then as a favor
to a beloved former student who, as a publisher, has neither
written nor taught philosophy. He was even more reticent about
giving public lectures. He gave a very successful one at my urging
at Harvard and a less successful one there four years later, and
only a few others, despite entreaties. He was also reluctant to
travel. From his middle years on he almost never ventured farther
from Williamstown than Pittsfield, Bennington, and North
Adams; but he did spend a sabbatical year in Rome.

From his behavior, one might think that he was timid, insecure,
and repelled by confrontation, criticism, or change. But anyone
who knew him knows that such an explanation is hardly even a
partial truth. Whatever his reasons for not traveling, one was
surely his distaste for the disruptions in his thinking that traveling
would produce: he needed uninterrupted mornings and a settled
environment. Whatever his discomfort at having to fend off at-
tacks on his thought, it was not criticism that he shunned but the
hostility of much of it. In a profession where reputation rests
upon the ability to cut up someone else's argument, even—one
sometimes suspects, especially—without understanding it, such
hostility is commonplace. In practice, professional philosophy,
where there is a concern for reputation, is but a species of prize
fighting, once removed from the bloody arena of what is called
sports by the fact that the combat is carried on with words rather
than fists and with rules drawn from the scholarly pursuits. If
Miller would have none of it, it was not that he risked losing but
that participation could not but debase and abuse thought, and
this he would not countenance in any instance. Miller's unwillingness to participate by writing and speaking in the affairs of his

profession is, as with his unwillingness to travel, best explained by his reverence for the sanctity of thought.

Of course, we who knew him wanted to believe that he could have held his own, even triumphed, if he had been willing to enter the fray. I remember how neatly he cut down one of the analytic sophists of the Harvard department with, "Oh, it's a word that's bothering you! Well, try this one ——! Or this ——! Maybe this one will do ——!" With no one word to attack, the poor man was for once left speechless. But the fact remains that Miller would not have come off well in most encounters. Despite his constant search for the right way to express himself, he could be cavalier, if not irresponsible, with words. He had his own vocabulary, as Whitehead did, but he mixed technical language with colloquial expressions, often rather quaint, from his upstate New York origins. His discourse, as well as his writing, was ornamented with literary quotations, often from Shakespeare and the poets and sometimes from the Catholic liturgy, in Latin. As his model for arguing was F. H. Bradley, his model for writing was Emerson—both quite out of fashion. But worst of all was the fact that when stripped of lush embodiments and reduced to bare quantifiable propositions which eliminated rich contexts and associations, what he had to say tended to make less sense and seemed less important or addressed to no current point of dispute. The student had to have faith that there was much more to what Miller was saying than the words that he employed could convey on any simple interpretation and a will to find out what that was. When, toward the end of his tenure, these were undercut by uncomprehending colleagues, his reputation on the Williams campus simply vanished and what should have been his crowning years were greatly compromised.

In view of the fact that philosophers as disparate as Wittgenstein and Heidegger, not to mention Kant and Hegel, can be turned into mush by the techniques of linguistic analysis and yet survive their dissectors, it is obligatory for anyone who would deal with the thought of a man of Miller's stature to make every possible effort to get beneath the linguistic obstacles to understanding. For the real problem in reading Miller only begins with the manner in which he expressed himself: most fundamentally, it is a matter of the level of his thinking. This is not something for which defining, translating expressions, and resolving ambiguities will suffice. As a young instructor he had much trouble being understood. James Bissett Pratt once said to him: "You seem to understand everything that I say, but I cannot understand anything that you say."

Although the remark was probably intended to contrast Pratt's meticulous expression with Miller's seemingly wanton use of language, it may be interpreted as indicating a limitation in Pratt's view: Miller was thinking at the profounder level. It was as with Hume and Kant: Kant, who had read little Hume, understood Hume well, but one wonders whether Hume could have understood Kant at all, even given the entire writings. Pratt, like Hume, was the better writer because what he had to say was simpler and required no unusual orientation in thought. Profundity is not unlike geological hardness, which is determined by scratchability: the higher degree belongs to the philosophical view that can comprehend the other. The problem of reading Miller is thus not merely a matter of diligent study but of a point of view, and that cannot be established by an explanation or an argument. Herein lies the difficulty not only in reading Miller but in reading philosophy generally, and Miller's concern for it pervaded his introductory course, "Types of Philosophy."

In casting about for the most accessible entry into the subject of what Miller's point of view or orientation in philosophy is, it should help to bear in mind that Miller's philosophy is at bottom a *philosophy of philosophy,* the sort of thing that emerges at the end of inquiry rather than at the beginning, as it did in fact in the history of philosophy with Hegel. It is no accident that Miller treated most of what he read, especially in contemporary philosophy, with a mixture of contempt and respect—contempt because of the arrogance of assertions without awareness of their dialectical foundation, and respect because these are essays of the human mind in establishing its own condition. Having discovered the concepts of ontological power that structure not only knowledge and the human mind but all human institutions, philosophers then spoil them by treating them as mere class names or descriptions or even as mere words.

This distinction between *philosophical* concepts and all other concepts separates Miller from his contemporaries in the profession. These are the concepts that, functioning as principles, organize thought in knowing, acting, and the being that depends on the agency of thought—the human self and all of its institutions. Miller referred to these as "constitutional concepts" and he maintained that they are the sole interest of philosophy. His courses in the "philosophy of" art, the state, history, etc., generally began by showing that there was a constitutional element in each for philosophers to attend to. He explained his use of "constitutional" by observing that political constitutions specify the principles for making laws rather than the specific laws themselves. In this respect the prohibition amendment was unconstitutional. We are of course all concerned with such concepts just as we use them; but philosophers deal with them systematically. The point is at least as old as Socrates, who recognized that the concepts of justice and virtue, when taken too simply, threatened political association and the ability to act in individuals. It was, of course, the point of Kant's categories. But it was not until Hegel that it became fully explicit and general. It is no accident that Miller treated the preface to *The Phenomenology of Mind* with special reverence.

This helps to explain why Miller was reluctant to publish. What he feared in publishing was not criticism, which he welcomed from students as well as associates in the profession. Criticism was in fact one of his categories. What he feared was the hostile criticism of those who did not recognize the fundamental difference between philosophical thought and other thinking. He was in this respect in the same predicament as Kant and Hegel and, for that matter, Plato. Miller rightly feared whoever would treat his thought as if it were *about* something—metaphysics in the now discredited sense. It is surely ironic, although not unexpected, that the current interest in Miller has produced expositors who would treat Miller as writing metaphysics in the manner of Paul Weiss and Charles Hartshorne.

Miller's basic point, then, is that certain concepts (e.g., causality), functioning as principles, by which they are often expressed (e.g., causality as "every event must have a cause"), are constitutional in thought (e.g., the sciences) and in being (e.g., practical activity). This is not new. Miller went further to maintain that these constitutional concepts are neither mere accidents nor inventions, nor elements in the psychology of the race, as Kant seems to suggest; nor are they eternal: they have a history, and this history is founded in their actual functioning in human life. Our conceptual systems shape up as they must that we might live by them. And this living is always local, finite, individual. They are constantly under a dialectical pressure for orderly revision, as Hegel and Bradley recognize, although without sufficient acknowledgment of the existential foundations of these demands. The dialectic is powerless to move except as the concepts are actually employed. The dialectic belongs to thought only as it is "at work in the world," to use Hegel's phrase; but this work is always done in the lives of actual individuals. What causality means today is a function of the role that it plays in actual scientific investigation. What a right is depends upon the needs and character of the society that establishes and enforces rights. Miller could not stress this point too strongly. It was of first importance—because not often seen—that the constitutional elements of actual life cannot be argued to, and have authority only in their continuity with the system of all such concepts as are formal or organizing in actual life.

This is why Miller continually stressed the historical (continuity in time) and the accidental (existential), which he exalted as categories, often asserting that he had added to the Kantian and Hegelian lists one more: the accidental. In more exuberant moments he sometimes referred to this category as "Madness," by which he meant something antithetical to reasoning or argumentation. And so it is: our existence today is structured by concepts that have developed historically in the face of such contingencies as war and famine and an unlimited frontier and the emergence of such technologies as electricity, television, and the computer. He was fond of Hegel's "Bacchic revel in which not a dancer is sober," which he often quoted in denying that the categories can be derived by reasoning. The categories danced but were not, as James described them, bloodless. Miller's commitment to the actual was manifest in a constant—too constant, for some—reiteration of the finitude of human processes, the "affirmation of the local," the here and now, to which he called attention by references to the instruments, things held in the hand, as it were, through which we act and know. He would shock freshmen by saying, "without the yardstick there is no distance between here and North Adams": distance is measured distance, not just extension. Eventually this came to be called the midworld—a world of instruments, including language and gestures, through which the ideal is manifest and articulated.

As originally conceived, the midworld was made up of objects, physical and ideal, that introduce structure or order by the interpretations placed upon them. A yardstick is a piece of lath with a special meaning by which it functions in the organization of the world that we know and act in. Ultimately, the midworld came to include the human body, for hands and eyes and muscles also function as instruments. The stress on the midworld was, I think, a natural consequence of his belief that what he had to say filled a space in idealism and saved it from lapsing into realistic affirmations of an absolute on one side or a thing-in-itself on the other, which he found equally inconsistent with idealism's basic principle. Miller intended an idealism without compromises.

Unfortunately, Miller's midworld seems to raise at least as many problems as Kant's schematism of the categories, to which it is related. Has he slipped into his own realism? Is this merely Dewey's instrumentalism, somewhat expanded? Does the mid-world have an ontological status? If we had no thermometers, would we still have body temperature? Such questions are of the kind that realists ask, and they seem to miss the point. Still, one wonders, has Miller done with the midworld what the absolute idealists did with thought in turning it into a thing or an object by naming it?

The answer here is to be found in holding fast to the funda-mental point that philosophers are concerned solely with the constitutional elements of active life. The task of philosophy is to facilitate, not prescribe, constitutional revision as required to maintain an orderly world and the self-control of finite selves. We get into philosophy because constitutional elements in our lives demand attention, because, as Miller expressed it, "we come to a point of systematic arrest" through a "constitutional disorder." We have information, but we cannot interpret it; we have oppor-tunities for action but not the required control: the line between appearance and reality is insecure. We have to advance another step if we are to maintain ourselves as active beings in an ever-changing world. That a philosopher makes the world more intel-ligible and by that enables us to better maintain a world in which we are able to act is the basis of any claim that he makes to objectivity. Otherwise all he has to offer are abstractions and arguments that belong only to the realm of ideas. "In philosophy," Miller often observed, "the objective is the object-[and subject]-defining." Philosophy that does not arise from the demands of the constitutional elements in the ways that we think in knowing and being (this includes human institutions as well as selves) is both irrelevant and irresponsible. Cut loose from these controls—this "environment"—philosophy becomes vagrant and irresponsible and falls easy prey to fads and fashions. Small wonder that when Miller's students went into philosophy professionally, they were never able to participate in its games, to their professional disad-vantage—but they were often superior teachers.

In his concern for thought at work in the world Miller is only restating the preface to the *Phenomenology*. But he goes much further. At first he added a stress on the concern to maintain control, in the spirit of Fichte: the world is as it must be that I may act in my own right. (*The Vocation of Man* was one of the readings in the introductory course.) The emphasis was on the local, unique individuality of each person's concern. As Miller came to recognize that this control is always exercised through instruments that we receive, create, and transmit to others, he came to recognize and stress the fact that the organizing or constitutional concepts work in the world through the instruments by which we control the world and pursue our purposes. Words, which are conveyed by sounds that differ only a little from grunts and snarls and odd configurations on paper, serve as instruments essential for the functioning of minds as minds and to their essential intercommunication. Yardsticks and calipers are transformed by interpretation from pieces of lath and shaped metal into instruments by which we organize space as we know and act in it. One cannot give an account of constitutional concepts without considering their foundation in the concern for control; and one cannot give an account of that control without recognizing the instruments by which that control is exercised. Such is Miller's mid-world—a world of instrumentalities, but emphatically not of *mere* instruments, means to ends, as in John Dewey's instrumentalism: these are vehicles of the ideal element in experience and being.

Obviously, Miller's thought developed out of the idealism that he encountered as a student at Harvard. He seems to have seen much that he could not let go of in the thought of W. E. Hocking and possibly Josiah Royce, whose last teaching year coincided with Miller's first but whose influence remained strong through Miller's graduate school years. But while these provided the power and direction of his thinking, the challenge to which his thought was directed seems not to have been idealism, but realism—the down to earth realism of the Catholic church, from which he had departed but which remained about him in his family, and especially the sophisticated realism of J. B. Pratt, under whom he taught at Williams. Miller, who respected practical men profoundly (while he admired sound scholarship and the possession of the knowledge of detail greatly, he distrusted intellectuals who were separated from the world and thereby from an essential condition of intellectual responsibility), could not have missed the appeal of a doctrine so natural to those who work with their hands and yet so unsatisfying for a philosophical mind. The bankruptcy of all the devices by which realists attempt to move from consciousness to an "external" world only to end in question-begging assumptions or dogmatic table thumping must have impressed upon him the urgency of reformulating the problem: we begin as realists—as selves in a world that is not our intention: our problem is not to explain or justify that realism, but to maintain it. The distinction between appearance and reality is constantly being threatened, but it cannot be maintained by a mere theory. For realism is itself an answer to a demand not made by objects or things or by the human psyche; nor is it given in privileged knowledge of some sort; realism is constitutional in human existence. And this demands dialectical support. Our problem is not to argue to an external world but to maintain the system of concepts by which we are able to identify and act in such a world. Miller's emphasis on the world-defining instrumentalities of his midworld only holds that dialectic to its task; and he who would turn the midworld into another object of whatever sort has missed Miller's very strong point.

Put at its simplest, we do not begin with the problem of arguing to a real world: we begin in the world and our problem is to maintain the modes of its apprehension and of our existence and practical effectiveness in it. Thus the concern for the dialectic of constitutional concepts which has been central in philosophy. But philosophers erred in taking them as abstract or abstracted ideas. We are in the actual world through the instruments by which we organize, articulate, and control the world: by these the constitutional concepts do their work. The items of Miller's midworld are indeed in the world; but they are in it as bearers of interpretation. They are the agents of the system of categories. A yardstick is not merely a device to determine dimensions or to settle an argument about relative sizes. It is a device by which we articulate and lay out space, as thermometers are devices by which we differentiate one quality from others and make comparisons within a quality. Coins are more than devices to work slot machines: they are instruments for the transfer of ownership and measures of economic value. By stressing the singularity of the entities of his midworld, Miller is only attempting to hold philosophers to their own foundations.

Miller's philosophy of philosophy will probably determine his place in the history of American philosophy. But it is not the reason why Miller is remembered by his students: they remember him for the power and depth of his thought on concrete issues— most notably for his ability to get beneath conflicting opposites to the concrete position that generates them and from which they are but abstractions. If we would honor him we must consider how what he held about philosophical thought and its special logic gave him his extraordinary capacity to open up, illuminate, and advance students' minds on all matters of concern. We might then better understand how it was that although at one time he held the record for former students in the graduate program at Harvard— in spite of his refusal to encourage anyone to go into the profession—he took greatest pride in his students (e.g., General Telford Taylor of the Nuremberg Trials) who had distinguished careers in the nonacademic world.

If further research is to be done, it thus would best not be as the taxonomic analysis that Miller despised so intensely that the editor of his collected essays felt obligated to forego essential bibliographical notations. Rather, it is to exhibit the inner logic of Miller's thought. I, for one, would greatly value an account of the way in which Miller's midworld functions to provide the depth and insight of his letters and conversations on topics of general interest. I suspect that Miller would have liked to see that too.

II
Some Basic Features of Miller's Philosophy

Acts and Necessity in the Philosophy of John William Miller

James A. Diefenbeck

Southern Illinois University

Introduction

THE philosophy expressed in the five volumes containing the work of John William Miller is at once original and daring, generated from a pious but revisionary attitude toward the historical past. Its signature is a colloquial and unpretentious style, both elegant and exact, and refreshingly pungent—but not without its difficulties even for the initiated. Its fundamental commitment is to the ultimate authority of the present, immediate, limited acts of embodied agents. The worlds of reality and appearance, of universals, and of history itself are seen as emerging from the unfolding of such acts. The main enemies contended against are on the one side radical empiricism, which holds that reality is centered in an inanimate world of objects existing independently of activity and thought, and on the other side a transcendent absolute unity also thought of as uninfluenced by human activities.

Acts of local control are the source of all else. "But in the living moment of assertion resides the true absolute. It describes no *fait accompli,* but an endeavor, and a procedure."[1] Yet this insurgency of the will would seem to face the charge of subjectivity, that is, the vagrancy and irresponsibility which characterize any act uncontrolled by anything other than itself. Such initiative autonomy appears to be achieved at the price of order and rationality since there is, by definition, nothing *initially* existing outside of itself which can fundamentally or completely determine it. The basic drive of Miller's philosophy is an attempt to solve this problem by showing how the immediate act has progressively civilized itself through an objectified reflection upon its own operation without appeal to an alleged absolute source of control entirely apart from human acts. In this way the gods were overthrown and a new order of control was generated by thought, but this revolutionary result "was achieved by adventures into the learning of action,

43

when local control projected a universal order and so invested the actual and present with the inherent power of declaring the unenvironed."[2] Through what specific operations have agents generated from their own resources such a connected rationality when this effort makes no appeal to the assumed existence of either an independently real nature or a transcendent divinity? What form has been taken by the attempt to rescue unenvironed acts from disorderly isolation?

The Self as Generating, and as Known through, Objects

The initial attack on this problem, worked out in *The Definition of the Thing*, attempts to indicate how our world of objects is not an independent existence but is, rather, generated by the acts of agents. The negative aspect of this argument demonstrates that, if our attitude is entirely passive or receptive, as it is seen to be by radical empiricism, no object could be known and no connected or ordered world could be generated. The positive side of this development points out that our own activity is ingredient in the very apprehension of objects and their ordered world. This general idea is, of course, not new. It is perhaps the central insight in Kant's account of our knowledge of nature. But what is new, and what Miller himself sees as his most original contribution, is the development of this idea, in terms not of changeless universal categories uninfluenced by voluntary human acts, but of limited and changeable acts of particular human agents.

These acts, crucial for our knowledge of nature, are those which generate "functioning objects." Such acts bring into existence an object, but one which is more than a merely encountered object in that it is an artifact, or an object which has been created by deliberate human agency. Further, such a functioning object, e.g., a yardstick or clock, has a significance beyond that of a tool, which is an artifact used as a means to a particular end. A yardstick is an artifact which itself controls and directs further action, such as measuring space, rather than itself being merely used and directed by such activity as a tool is used. A functioning object exists in what is termed "the midworld," a meeting ground of object and act, but it is in an act which has generated this intermediate territory. To treat a functioning object merely as a tool, that is as a means to a particular practical end, is a desecration of it, for its proper function is to provide a standard for further action, such as measuring objects or telling time.

We act in creating a yardstick; this functioning object then enables us to move on, through an activity ordered by it, to establish our knowledge of a world of objects and thus, in a way, that very world itself. The yardstick represents a limited act or assertion, yet this very limitation is the means by which we can expand our activity and our knowledge, when guided by this standard, in a possibly infinite progression. The functioning object thus makes possible a distinction between the real and the apparent, for instance the differentiation of the measured or real distance between two objects from the merely observed or apparent distance between them. A similar extension of the limited act produces universal concepts, which transcend the particular and limited but only because they are seen not as merely encountered foreign existents, unrelated to the knower's activity, but as forms generated by his limited activity itself. This activity, employing functioning objects, also generates the continuous and the infinite. A yardstick, for instance, is finite, but by its repeated use in measuring we generate the continuum of universal space. Thus an activity, directed by a functioning object, can move in an unlimited extension toward the infinite.

The infinite and the universal represent thus, not worlds completely different from the finite and the particular which somehow shed their orders upon this immediate existence, but rather unlimited extensions of activity as a particular act generates, and then uses, a yardstick or clock. This is a powerful idea, for it shows how the universal can be generated from our direct acts and how it can apply to the particular and relate it to the universal order. Another way of putting this priority of the act is to say that our acts are "unenvironed," that is, are generative of the environment rather than being determined by it. We cannot, however, "know" a yardstick as we can know particular objects through perception, for its status comes not from being perceived but from our *assertion* that it is a functioning object. A yardstick represents not merely an object or an artifact (although it is both and is used in our generation of knowledge of objects), but our act, which itself gives it its significance.

The Definition of the Thing works out these ideas in technical detail in relation to the definition of objects, classes, signs, and to what Miller calls "the ontological proof," wherein the assertion of a concept justifies itself and establishes its own reality. The volumes representing Miller's later thought, while not abandoning these ideas, exhibit a shift in the center of interest. This different emphasis can be located by following a change in the way in which the subject's self-knowledge is presented.

In some passages subject and object are spoken of as being in a reciprocal relationship; that is, knowledge of self appears only as correlative with the emergence of our knowledge of objects. "These two terms [mind and body] are strictly correlative."[3] "The objectified act is the basis of all objectivity and all subjectivity too."[4] Elsewhere the position is stated even more forcefully: "Objectivity is the other side of selfhood. Only in objectivity is the self real to itself, self-maintaining" (PC, p. 163). And in the volume devoted to psychology there is an assertion that self-knowledge requires the identity of all minds in their knowledge of nature. ". . . there is no way of knowing other minds *except through the objects of nature*. . . . But while the road leads through nature, it is through nature as a whole, not through its parts."[5] "*Hence another self is another such world of experience* identical with one's own in all essentials" (DP, p. 167).

Our knowledge of ourselves is thus presented as depending upon, and as being elicited by, our development of a knowledge of nature. But as interest shifts from the part our acts play in the apprehension of objects toward a concern with acts themselves, the primary focus of attention shifts from nature to history.

The Self Known through Constitutional Utterance

One way of noting this shift is found in the extension of the reference which is given to the term "utterance." This expression refers to an activity which can establish constitutional or categorical forms. Such utterances appear initially as functioning objects such as yardsticks and clocks, but particularly in the later thought the range of activity referred to is expanded. The general term "utterance" comes to be used in reference not merely to measuring devices such as yardsticks and clocks but also to words, gestures, buildings, and the creations of the arts. Thus this term has a very wide range of application and would seem to include nearly everything which initiative activity can produce. In fact even the body is spoken of as "*the absolute artifact*, that is, it is the artifact that in its functioning creates all other artifacts and symbols. It is the absolute *actuality*, that is, the union of form and content in functioning" (M, p. 46).

Now the Parthenon or Chartres (both frequently referred to in the texts) are objects, artifacts, and at least in some sense functioning objects, as are yardsticks. But they would seem to function in a dimension radically different from that in which yardsticks operate. The yardstick is the product of an activity and it directs a further activity. The activity it directs is one which seeks some element of permanence in objects in order to establish a truth about them. The function of the Parthenon is also to direct activity, but in a very different way. It leads us not to a knowledge of objects, as does the yardstick, but to an understanding of subjects, and most particularly to other selves following heterogeneous modes of thought and feeling and action rather than to the identical minds which are said to emerge from our study of nature.

Further, if the body itself is an utterance, its operation involves much more than does that of the inanimate yardstick, for it is alive and self-changing as the yardstick is not. And if words are also utterances, they are very different from utterances such as the Parthenon since, as uttered, they may be very fleeting, and they certainly have no weight or size or many of the other characteristics of artifactual objects. And again, while words such as those used in mathematics can lead us to knowledge of objects as do yardsticks, other words, such as those used in poetry or in the formulation of concepts of action, do not refer to objects; they reveal, rather, the feelings or thoughts of subjects. In this way, much of this expanded range of utterances operates very differently from yardsticks and clocks. And such aesthetic and conceptual utterances may well lead us to the apprehension of other subjects whose actions, feelings, and thoughts are very different from our own. And it is these very relationships with subjects different from oneself which begin to establish the self in a new dimension.

In this dimension the self is presented not merely as it is when revealed through the reciprocal relation of subject and object, where it is differentiated from objects or from not-selves but is otherwise unspecified. In this new relationship a self appears as individual and unique, just in proportion to its differentiation from other unique individuals. The identity of all minds, which emerges as the self-knowledge produced when the problem is knowing objects, is succeeded by the differentiation among minds which emerges from historical study of the past. And this diversification presents a new problem. How can the various, and often incompatible, acts and governing concepts of individual subjects, or of historical periods, be related to each other? This problem requires us to move from the connection of different entities by a permanent element common to all (as the yardstick relates different distances through a common unit) to the relation of different entities, here appearing as diverse individual subjects or historical periods, *in terms of their very differences themselves.*

The midworld of functioning objects may be, as Miller himself thinks, his most original contribution, but it seems to me that this presentation of the theory of history as a fundamental dimension of thought or, as he puts it, a constitutional category, is his most memorable and profound accomplishment. His aim is to establish the act in this historical dimension as a fundamental category of thought, a constituting metaphysical reality, that is, one without which the self as agent cannot know itself. And, in my judgment, the most moving passages as well as the most profound ideas appear apropos of this problem of historical thought which is seen to encompass philosophy itself. Miller is at his best in such passages as the various analyses of skepticism and of its relation to the naive individual and to the dogmatist. And the essay "The Ahistoric Ideal,"[6] where he traces the idea of static unity as it rises to high tide in the thought of Plato, Boethius, and Augustine, and then ebbs, manifests a depth and a soaring eloquence that reach beyond any of the studies centered on objects.

Self-Knowledge through History

History is presented as occurring apropos of the limited, present, and immediate act, for, "as self-maintenance the present is absolute" (PH, p. 128). The particular act, as local control, is the source from which both development and knowledge of the self proceed. "One reaches the point of no argument, not in a timeless axiom, but in a past deed or experience that has been organizing and is not now to be questioned without a collapse of all control and identity" (DP, p. 176). But this self-assertion, generated from passionate egoism, is able to generate history only because it is not static and completely self-assured. One source of such disquietude, appearing in "the desperate assertion of a limited and unfinished will" (PC, p. 36), is an agent's realization that his commitment and his act have come into existence from a past and so cannot be adequately known in their *immediate* occurrence, as an object is known. A present belief or act can be brought into further self-awareness only through a process of self-discovery moving beyond immediacy. This expansion of self-knowledge is achieved by finite particular acts which explore a past characterized by dated time. And all such acts, present and past, are subject to error and correction; "to avoid error is to avoid history, and to have no constitutional place for error is to leave the historical undefined and the dateless truth as monstrous arbitrariness" (PH, p. 13). And all acts are original and unique; absence of originality implies absence of an act.

The study of the past is launched by the obscurity of the present self. One occasion for this is a conflict within the self, and a particular source of such conflict can be a breakdown or opposition appearing in the moral world. This is not merely a specific practical difficulty but is rather a conflict within, or an inadequacy of, the governing form of order being followed. It is a *categorical* breakdown, for no such ordering structure is either completely ordered or completely disordered. Appeal to the past appears as the effort to maintain a present position, to certify it, although this investigation discovers that its real intent is to revise the very position whose attempt at self-maintenance launched the historical investigation. Self-maintenance is made possible and is enhanced by a study of the past because of the self-reformation to which this investigation may lead. Present willfulness thus appeals to the past in order to understand itself and, through self-revision, to preserve effective action in the present.

Miller notes that despite the cognitive priority of the idea of history as a category, historically it appeared subsequently to the idea of nature. "It was reason, and not action, wherein man first joined the universal and the free." And again: "The idea of history waits upon the idea of nature and rises to authority only when time has been lost in the invariant, and when action has been made unintelligible by universal order. The sense of time is original, but the status of time as a constitutional factor of experience is derivative" (*PH*, p. 17).

These passages indicate that the first efforts of agents moving to civilize their actions appeal to the invariant order of nature as the corrective to their own disordered variability. And it is only when men discover that this appeal to the static as an absolute definition of reason leaves no place for the very activity which originated this investigation that they begin to recognize that both the act, as a dimension of change in time, and history, as a mode of knowledge, are categorical or constituting forms of reality and of knowledge. Thus today history has become the dominant category wherein man finds or, more accurately, creates himself. Man can act, as this is distinguished from animal reaction, only because he has taken into account what has been done. To be in history is to see the present as historical fate, although what "fate" implies in this context involves some not fully explored problems.

The urgency of our connection with the past, itself raises the problem of the form which such a connection with the past is to take. The historical acts which are our concern are "the great acts that mark the moments of our enlarged energies" (*PH*, p. 85). These are the acts which, as establishing categorical or constitutional forms, sustain a world. They might be termed categories on the move. Consideration of such past acts seeks to disclose the act, "in its temporal heritage, in its antecedents and consequent involvements" (*PC*, p. 132). History is the story of the consequences of our commitments and of the revisions of outlook which follow from such passionate allegiances to any particular concept of general order. Historical study is concerned with our purposes, less in relation to their execution or enactment than to the process which revises them. "The essence of a purposive act is not only that it proceeds from a general program but also that it requires the revision of the program in the interests of which it is undertaken" (*PH*, p. 33). The knowledge of the present, as this is concerned with acts, appears only as we see the present in relation to "a previous condition from which we have emerged, which we now repudiate but do not disavow as the ancestor of our present self-identity" (*PH*, p. 95).

The two ontological categories or articulations of finitude which emerge from the study of history are "commitment," or the act following a particular directing form, and "the relatively static," that is, a guiding form which is more enduring and compelling than particular purposes but which does not have the eternal unchanging normative status of an ahistoric ideal. Thus we have history only where there is some order, but only where such an order has come into existence and has been marked by a date as occurring in a particular context, and where it is subject to modification. History is the criticism of the systematic and emphasizes, not the static quality or completeness of an assumed order, but rather its position in a moving sequence. One consequence of this is that history cannot be controlled, for were it controlled by something outside of itself, it would lose the name of action. "Action is in principle unpredictable because it generates the relatively static orders within which all prediction occurs" (*PH*, p.105). While physics invokes the ideally complete, history invokes the ideally incomplete. Thus history changes in the direction of diversity and variety.

This account of the historical mode of thought is given a thumbnail portrait in the following passage: "In sum, history is action, and action is will, and will is both purpose and the revision of purpose, and the revision of purpose is freedom, having no other end than the maintenance of action itself. . . . All history can teach at last is that there *is* history" (*PH*, pp. 35–36).

"Necessity," "Truth," and "Absolute" as Equivocal Terms

Such a summary, even though borrowing Miller's words, expressions, and even extended (and sometimes unacknowledged) quotations is very thin milk compared with the richness, variety, and pungency of the original presentation, nearly every page of which cries out for quotation. Since the ideas come out in their full animation only in the volumes themselves, I should like, as an alternative to continuing with a more detailed exposition of the structure of historical thought, to turn to an examination of three terms which appear in the texts with some frequency and which, because they are open to different interpretations, present certain difficulties and discrepancies in regard to the fundamental concepts developed. These terms are "necessity," "truth," and "absolute." The problem emerges, I think, because of the intrusion of the mode of thought appropriate for a knowledge of objects into the treatment of historical relations among acts.

The immediate problem which faces the attempt to understand history as a study of acts is what is termed "subjectivity." This indicates an act which is self-initiated and self-directed but which seems to have no form beyond this self-assertion so that it appears as haphazard and fickle because it is unrelated to, and is thus unordered by, anything other than itself. As Wordsworth says,

> Me this uncharted freedom tires;
> I feel the weight of chance desires.

Miller frequently appeals to necessity as a counter to the indeterminacy, or lack of control and order, exhibited by any isolated act, a counter by which such an act's vagrancy may possibly be overcome. He generally applies the term to those acts which establish constitutional or categorical forms, that is, the fundamental structures or armatures of a world. If an act is necessary it must be done. In this way it is given some status in contrast to those acts which are merely subjective or optional and have no such supporting reassurance.

Allied with the idea of necessity as it applies to acts is the idea of truth. In relation to acts, truth appears as a norm, that is, a mode or concept of action which should or must be followed. What force of control can the related ideas of necessity and truth actually establish in regard to our acts?

Necessity finds its ideal cognitive meaning in the analytical realm of deduction; here, in the relation of premise and conclusion, we can demonstrate an absolute certainty of relationship or a necessary truth. Such a necessary truth represents a passivity of the knower before what is known; it cannot be other than it is; thus the idea of an unquestionable necessity or an unchallengeable truth is achieved. A less certain but more objective necessity (objective in the sense of referring to an encountered world beyond the knower's control) appears in what may be termed practical or empirical necessity; here we are concerned with a commonsense observation about something like the sun's regular rising or a more rigorously established scientific law such as the law of gravity, both of which are based on encountered regular orders of perception which are at once beyond the knower's control and are regular or exceptionless (at least to date), but which could conceivably be different in the future.

In both of these forms of necessary truth the essential mode of apprehension is the passivity of the knower before something not in his control, and the cognitive content of this passivity takes the form of permanence or of the static. Thus it is in deductive and in empirical thought that the terms necessity and truth gain their cognitive status. This means that we can explain exactly what necessity means in these two areas and can provide a method whereby we can determine whether any particular assertion is, or is not, a deductive or an empirical truth.

Can these terms, which appear as essential in our knowledge of objects, be properly applied to acts? When a person says that his philosophy or a norm he intends to follow is true or that a certain act is morally necessary "in that he can do no other," what legitimate meaning can necessity and truth actually have in this context? The person who holds an act morally necessary does not intend to mean that he is physically capable of doing only this act and no other, for in this case he would not be morally responsible for his act. When an agent holds that his act or a category he asserts is necessary or is true, or is a necessary truth, all that he can legitimately mean is 1) that such an action or thought is in his control, 2) that he is resolved to act or to think in this way, and 3) that in his judgment it is the best way of acting or thinking open to him. The problem is how such a rational or connected judgment as to the best is to be established. If one appeals to truth or necessity one is using terms which derive their cognitive force from the objective realm; this compulsion requires that the knower be passive before something not in his control and that the entity known exhibit an enduring or static form. If, in these terms, an act were true or necessary, it would not be an act self-initiated by the agent concerned, but an effect whose source or cause would be elsewhere so that the agent would disappear in the truth or necessity established. Also, because of the permanence required by truth and necessity, such an act or category, if established as true, would hold as an eternal verity for all persons.

And in a more practical vein, my assertion that a certain category is true or necessary does not of itself actually force you to adopt it whereas my assertion, backed by a demonstration, of a deductive or empirical truth does force you to accept it. Similarly, my assertion that I find a certain act morally necessary does not mean that you either do, or must, find it morally necessary. Such usages of truth and necessity are either illegitimate, in that they propose to give a status to an act which they cannot actually establish, or, if they were actually to establish a presumed act as necessary, such an act would lose the name of action, that is, its status as a self-initiated mode of behavior.

These difficulties in the appeal to truth and necessity in order to establish the legitimacy of our acts, mean, not that the problem this appeal seeks to solve does not exist and is not important, but rather that its solution cannot actually be achieved through the modes of thinking indicated by these terms, which find effective use in either deductive thought or in our knowledge of objects. The question of justification of a subjective act or category is insistent. It arises as the problem of how to overcome what is termed "subjectivity," that is, acts which are unordered or irresponsible because they are isolated and unconnected with anything beyond themselves. Instinctive acts do not require any such control since they are done immediately and without consideration of alternatives; but when agents develop awareness of alternative acts, the question of choice among possible actions appears with some urgency. The appeal to what Miller calls the ahistoric ideal represents one (unsuccessful) attempt to deal with this problem. The decisive question is whether solution of the problem of ordering activity is to be established by appeal to some passive dimension other than truth and necessity, whatever this dimension might be, or whether such order is to be achieved within the active and subjective realm itself.

It seems to me that Miller's philosophy takes this latter alternative and that his theory of history elaborates this mode for generating order in a very detailed and convincing way. And it is because of the range and power of this historical mode of order that the references to necessity, truth, and the absolute appear only as surface blemishes, occasioned in my estimation by the intrusion of the forms used in the description of objects into the reflective realm. Let me indicate a few examples of this possible intrusion, not by way of criticizing the central philosophy itself, but in order to discourage certain misinterpretations which these expressions might suggest. I will first cite certain statements which seem to indicate an objective use of the terms involved and then other formulations which bring the significance of the terms into closer accord with the governing insight of Miller's position, which is centered in historical thought.

Necessity, for example, seems to appear on one hand with its full objective force: "the authority of criticism depends on the necessity of those structures in accordance with which criticism operates" (*PC,* p. 68). Or again: "The solution of any conflict, or rather its resolution, lies in realizing the necessity of the conflict" (*PC,* p. 71). The statement, "Necessary connection is a tautology" (*PC,* p. 126), suggests that all connections are necessary as does the assertion, "The history of philosophy is the record of such necessary conflicts" (*PC,* p. 70). But on the other hand, and counter to such interpretations, the status of necessity seems to be absorbed by, or to be reduced to, activity as indicated by the following statements: "The necessary remains arbitrary, or mere postulate, until it has been derived" (*PH,* p. 181). "All that is necessary—all that is possible—is *some* systematic issue" (*PH,* p. 189). This would eliminate the possibility that any particular position is necessary. And finally there is a passage in which the necessary and the absolute are explicitly dissolved in the agent's acts. "Only in the discovery of some fatal threat to himself in the framework of his inheritance can he discover freedom. There alone does he confront a necessary and an absolute problem, one proposed by himself and suffered in himself. . . . Freedom is . . . the revision of the basis of choice" (*PC,* p. 25). Here necessity is seen as enclosed in, and as generated by, the agent's activities.

References to truth as being in a positive relation to acts are less frequent than are such references to necessity and the absolute, although there are intimations of such a relationship. The statement, "There can be truth only where there are no final truths" (*PC,* p. 21), suggests this as does, "Truth is an enterprise, perpetually unfinished" (*PC,* p. 30). Here the truth may not be final, but it does seem to have some bearing on action. However the dominant note is an attack on truth as providing any ultimate or adequate standard of action. In the following quotation the commitments which dominate a historical period are presented not as truths but as myths. "Show me any mind of a time and I will show what truth-tellers call a myth. Action and the springs of action end as no part of the truth" (*PH*, p. 153). "If one wants history, then a self-revision of totalities cannot be avoided. And no such revision is a truth. It often appears as an assault on truth, on the assumptions that regulate the truths we tell" (*PH*, p. 152). Here the truth appears as no final cognitive or metaphysical element. And in the following quotation truth is presented, in its guise of permanence, as directly inimical to acts: "Far from making us free, the 'truth' has not even been comfortable in allowing us to exist at all, let alone gods and heroes" (*PH*, p. 154).

A divided attitude also makes its appearance in relation to the absolute when this term is used to provide an assurance of the superiority of one activity or value over others. Acts and values are various and possibly conflicting, whereas the absolute, thought of in the objective mode, is one and changeless so that it seems to provide a reliable standard and guide. But this attractive picture encounters fundamental difficulties.

The first function of an absolute, when appealed to by an agent contemplating action, is to establish or to fortify a determination to perform a particular act; but no passive relation can actually do this, for any agent must himself initiate his acts. And no inanimate ideal can itself initiate its enactment. The second function of an absolute, which appears when acts have advanced beyond those determined by instinct because alternative possibilities of action have made their appearance, is to guide choice among alternatives. But an absolute in the objective mode derives its cognitive force from both its changeless uniqueness and our passive or receptive attitude toward it. Yet any complete passivity before an absolute (required because the absolute is thought to be both single and all-inclusive) would destroy the agent's essential self-initiating activity, at least in regard to his determination of his guiding norms.

It is perfectly possible to assume the uniqueness of the absolute; yet any such assumption almost inevitably seems to be challenged, particularly when an explicit, and so useful, formulation is attempted, since this seems almost inevitably to elicit other different formulations. Any attempt to exchange dogmatic acceptance of any one of these for an ordered certification of it calls for the establishment of a relationship among these particular interpretations of the absolute. Such an ordering can come only from an agent who, although he may be following a governing absolute in the objective mode, is also concerned with the justification of his formulation of this absolute; this requires its relation with other

particular interpretations of the absolute—and so we are brought
to the very domain of historical thought which, through its relationships, dissolves the assumed timeless jurisdiction of any particular conception of the absolute. This reflective operation may
well lead to the development of new governing concepts so that it
becomes evident that the establishment of today's absolute does
not preclude that tomorrow's may be different from it.

Both interpretations of the absolute, as unified and changeless,
and as a limited and changing function, seem indicated by various
apparently opposed passages we can examine. In one statement
the absolute appears to be formulated in an objective sense: "Criticism . . . requires final and absolute standards" (PC, p. 35). In line
with this there are other assertions: "You can't acquire goals or
ideals. You can learn what goal you want, but you must have it
initially" (DP, p. 187). "End and beginning share a common authority, and the end has none with which the beginning was not
endowed" (M, p. 8). This relation between beginning and end
does hold between a premise and a deductive conclusion, but can
hardly be said to hold necessarily between one act and a later quite
different act, for here an expansion beyond the first act or position may well be indicated. In these quotations a governing absolute seems to be beyond change.

Yet in opposition to this seemingly atemporal interpretation of
the absolute, other more eloquent passages recognize the derivative, historical, and changing form of absolutes. "The static absolute is the obliteration of the finite. History is the preservation of
the finite in the revision of self-defining absolutes. . . . All absolutes are doomed, but not by the intellect which cannot so much as
propose them. They are doomed by history which is the process
which reveals them and so overpasses any one of them, and all of
them" (PC, p. 145). And finally there is a passage whose power
demands its inclusion. "There are no remote finalities, but there
are present ones, hidden in the living reality of any actual deed,
and compelling just in the measure that the deed drives onward
with persistent power. For the bankruptcy of finite deeds can get
clear only as they are first desperately undertaken and the illusion
of final and static satisfaction thereby disclosed. As a result, one is
thrown back upon some intrinsic validity of the will itself, not for a
certification of its value by some result external and accidental to
it. We can only assert value, we cannot *attain* it or *prove* it as an
incident to our own selfhood, or to our running experience in this
world or another"(PC, p. 37).

In these interpretations of truth, necessity, and the absolute, and of the opposition between an objective use which emerges in our attempt to know *things,* and an historical use which illuminates the economy of agents developing in time, it is clear that the historical interpretation is central to Miller's philosophy. However these lingering intimations of the possibility of an objective buttressing of the asserted values and categories which structure our worlds are essentially illegitimate and, in a small way, tend to confuse the legitimate effort to find a method for ordering activity, not by an appeal beyond activity to either an independent empirical world, or to a transcendent static absolute, but to activity's own moving processes as it expands and develops itself.

Conclusion

These five volumes of Miller's work provide what seem to me to be a highly original and a successful effort to analyze and to explore the problem of how we are to control our own acts in an ordered or connected way; and the answers they propose in terms of a historical world of self-controlled and self-related conceptually known acts place them still today on the very frontier of thought. The caveats raised here represent no more than an effort to blow away a speck of dust upon the surface.

Such an attempt at revision is in accord with Miller's idea of history as constitutional self-revision. Whether or not he would accept these particular emendations is beyond knowing. But I do know that contact with him many years ago in Williams College first awakened my mind and opened the door of philosophy; and his thought ever since has been a corrective and an inspiration. There is one passage in which Miller himself describes this happy and crucial process of transmission: "I come then to the idea that one's first sense of the actual occurs in this recognition of persons in whom one finds satisfaction of some sort. There, in some presence, one finds both oneself and one's world" (*DP,* p. 176). I have every confidence that his thought will assume a historic place in the wider world as it already has for those of us who were fortunate enough to experience these ideas clothed in the radiance of his genial and commanding presence. I can do no better in closing than to repeat the words of George Brockway, to whom we owe so much for his labors in bringing into print these otherwise inaccessible ideas: "Of all of the men of his time whom I have known, he was the wisest, and the justest, and the best."[7]

Notes

1. J. W. Miller, *The Paradox of Cause and Other Essays* (New York: Norton, 1978), p. 41. Hereafter, *PC*, with page references cited in the text.

2. J. W. Miller, *The Midworld of Symbols and Functioning Objects* (New York: Norton, 1982), p. 81. Hereafter, *M*, with page references cited in the text.

3. J. W. Miller, *The Definition of the Thing* (New York: Norton, 1980), p. 151.

4. J. W. Miller, *The Philosophy of History with Reflections and Aphorisms* (New York: Norton, 1981), p. 185. Hereafter, *PH*, with page references cited in the text.

5. J. W. Miller, *In Defense of the Psychological* (New York: Norton, 1983), p. 167. Hereafter, *DP*, with page references cited in the text.

6. In *Paradox of Cause,* pp. 130–60.

7. George P. Brockway, "John William Miller," *The American Scholar* 49 (1980): 240.

The Fatality of Thought

Henry W. Johnstone, Jr.

The Pennsylvania State University

THAT John William Miller had any reservations about the philosophy of Hegel was not obvious from his lectures in Philosophy 1–2 at Williams College, at least when I attended these lectures. In Philosophy 1–2 the controlling concept of "The Fatality of Thought" seemed, from the point of view of a young instructor systematically schooled to spurn Hegel, to illuminate the hitherto obscure mechanism of Hegelian dialectic. It was only when stressing "the moment," as he did especially both in courses other than Philosophy 1–2 and in his writing and conversation, that Miller expressed what amounted to a doubt of the finality of the Hegelian system.[1]

Philosophy 1–2 was called "Types of Philosophy." That Miller's Harvard teacher William Ernest Hocking had published a book under the title *Types of Philosophy*[2]—a book in which Miller is thanked in the preface—is clearly no coincidence, although Miller would no doubt have wanted to base his own version of the elementary philosophy course on types even if Hocking's book had not existed. (In his introductory lecture in 1947, he gave some arguments for choosing to base his elementary course on types rather than the history or the problems of philosophy. On the problems approach, he said: "Such an approach seduces you into opinions to which you are not entitled. Or it seduces instructors to discuss problems—for example, causality—where no profitable conclusion can be reached within the little time allotted.")[3]

Hocking's book was one of the main textbooks for the course, although it does not cover all the types that Miller lectured about, and includes material that he sometimes did not use in Philosophy 1–2. Hocking was supplemented by readings from representatives of the various types. Of the types that Miller treated in this course and that were also featured in Hocking's book, the first was the protophilosophy that introduced both the book and the course—a point of view that both teachers called "spiritualism." (I daresay that owing to the associations of this word with arcane doings, neither man could have been altogether happy about using it; but if there was a more felicitous alternative, no one has yet pointed it out. "Animism" is close, but lacks the necessary reference to action. "Panpsychism" denotes a theory, but spiritualism is emphatically not theoretical.)

The fatality of thought (here I drop the capitalization to avoid giving the impression that the phrase was a technical term or the name of a doctrine) figures as the decisive difference between Hocking's treatment of the types of philosophy and Miller's treatment of them. Hocking presents his types as primarily a list of alternative points of view. The arguments favoring each type are given, and each is subjected to criticism. But apart from spiritualism, "the protophilosophy," they can presumably be taken up in any order, and none prefigures a necessary sequel. In other words, Hocking's list of types is without historical context—it is, to use a term that Miller was fond of (but might possibly have refrained from using to characterize Hocking's textbook)— "ahistoric."[4] For Miller himself, on the other hand, something like an ideal history is played out in the transitions that lead from one type to its sequel or sequels. The point is that there *are* transitions. For example, naturalism[5] is seen as the necessary outcome of spiritualism.

The development of naturalism from spiritualism occurs as an outcome of the spiritualistic understanding of all events as purposive. This means that they ae all understood as acts of an agent. The idea of the human subject emerges as that of an agent among agents. Agents can act upon objects; and they can do so with varying degrees of success and failure. Success in dealing with objects depends on the correct assessment of their natural properties. You cannot handle an axe as you do a spade. You cannot handle clay as you do bronze. So the region of nature begins to emerge—a region ordered by relations among objects and among the properties of objects. Teleological explanations of events begin to recede in importance. The transition from spiritualism to naturalism is underway.

The sketch I have just made encapsulates two or three weeks of lectures. These lectures cover many aspects of spiritualism, and have the net effect of rendering plausible a point of view that might have seemed quaint, archaic, and superstitious. Miller's chief concern with any point of view on which he touched was to render it plausible—that is to say, to evoke the conditions under which the point of view necessarily arises rather than treating its appearance as the result of a spontaneous, arbitrary, and probably self-serving fabrication. It is, he thought, only our ability to recognize an alien point of view as in this way plausible that can save us from violent confrontations.[6] But it was not only the points of view in themselves that Miller sought to display as necessary and thus plausible; he also wanted to show that the *transition* from a point of view to its successor was in the same way also plausible. This was Miller's unique contribution to a study of the types of philosophy. An example of this contribution is the account of the transition between spiritualism and naturalism that I have outlined above. Such a transition obeyed what Miller called "a fatality of thought." "One philosophizes," Miller said, "when one discovers that there is a kind of fatality in a given position—that such a position is unstable."[7] To philosophize is to engage in revision that necessarily includes self-revision.[8]

The notes available to me do not make a great deal of use of the phrase "fatality of thought" that I can document. But I am sure I am not deluding myself in thinking that Miller used it fairly often in the period from 1948 to 1952, when I was attending his lectures—lectures on which I now unfortunately lack my own notes. (I do have the 1950–1951 notes of Joseph Fell, to which I shall have occasion to refer.) But it is not a momentous issue how often Miller actually used the expression "the fatality of thought." That was perhaps his most picturesque phase for what lay behind philosophical transitions, but it is clear that he used other phrases as well, speaking for example of "necessity," of "the career of thought," and of "what is in the cards."

In this article I shall concentrate on four transitions that Miller regarded as illustrating the fatality of thought; namely, spiritualism to naturalism, naturalism to subjective idealism, subjective idealism to realism, and realism to skepticism. There is much that I omit. The move through which spiritualism and naturalism combine to give rise to dualism does not seem to me to illustrate a necessity of the same order as the other transitions I have listed; and I am not at all sure that Miller himself thought that it did.[9] The later positions studied in the course—the "post-skeptical positions"—do not very clearly manifest the fatality, except possibly as contributing to the development of objective idealism. It is not going too far to say that the fatality of thought belonged to Philosophy 1 more than it did to Philosophy 2.

"The act declares its own environment." I have no record or even memory that Miller ever said this, but he might have. This Milleresque pronouncement is in any event a serviceable way to express the fatality that leads from spiritualism to naturalism. The environment declared by the act—as the agent becomes more sophisticated in his understanding of the conditions that govern

his success or failure—is nature. For it is within nature that the
responsible act falls. In the beginning, perhaps, the act was not
seen as environed. Was it felt as a pure spontaneity? If so, it could
not have been responsible. Indeed, it could not even have been
articulated as an *act*. The very concept of an *act* implicates nature.

"The act declares its own environment" is not an argument.
The spiritualist does not argue his way into naturalism. Miller was
always ready to present the arguments that became possible once
the various types had emerged—arguments, for example, for the
existence of God formulated within a sophisticated articulation of
spiritualism that could not have appeared until naturalism was
already on the scene—spiritualism, that is, in the specific form of
"super-naturalism"—but the emergence of the types themselves
was not occasioned by arguments. In Miller's scheme of things,
philosophical arguments played a minor role; they were a sort of
technical elaboration of a deeper process. When Miller outlined
the standard arguments it was usually, I felt, with a mild sense of
amusement. He was willing to impart to his students that familiarity with the textbook arguments generally expected of philosophy students; perhaps he felt obligated to provide budding
philosophers with the tools of their trade; but in his own opinion
these arguments didn't amount to much. And yet on the other
hand, the language in which Miller criticized positions to expose
their fatal flaws was argumentation of a sort, and this Miller took
quite seriously.

What I am trying to describe in using the phrase "The act
declares its own environment" is a *transition*. But the process does
not come to a halt with the mere emergence of the act's environment. Nature and the act are an unstable pair; they cannot coexist
in mutual externality, except in the deliberately contrived standoff
that Miller treated under the rubric of "dualism." As a theoretical
proposal, this standoff does not, as I said before, seem to me to
exhibit the nontheoretical urgency of a genuine fatality of
thought. That urgency is much better exhibited in the relation
between the act and its natural environment. The environment in
question turns out to be deadly, as unsupportive of the act as a
chlorine atmosphere would be of life. For naturalism reduces the
act to a necessary consequence of its causal antecedents, thus
destroying its freedom. So the full transition between spiritualism
and naturalism must be described by saying "The act declares its
own environment—and thereby perishes."

"[Nature] is a necessity of thought."[10] But naturalism, the claim
that nature has no environment,[11] is not the final type. To intro-

duce its successor (assuming that dualism was not its rightful successor), Miller was fond of using Emerson's little book on nature. In the sixth chapter, "Idealism," Emerson considers a variety of ways in which nature can appear as a spectacle. He mentions the effects of rides in balloons and railway cars, and of looking at the world between one's legs. "The least change in our point of view gives the whole world a pictorial air."[12] But the picture reveals not only the pictorial quality of nature but also the stability of the person who views it. The subject has emerged as the environment of nature.

If it were only unusual ways of looking at the world that made it into a spectacle, the naturalist might be able to dismiss as an aesthetic aberration the phenomenon Emerson instances—one which could no doubt be brought within the framework of a naturalistic psychology of perception. But science itself—the very medium through which nature is articulated—also reduces the latter to a spectacle. All that science can know of nature must appear within sense-experience; it can know no reality *behind* sense-experience. Nature, from the point of view delineated by Emerson, is thus no more than a spectacle played out in our experience.

To most readers of this article, the scenario I am sketching will be far too familiar to be interesting. Subjective idealism, especially at the hands of Berkeley, does in fact emerge essentially in the way Miller said it did. That the naturalism which Berkeley attacked was in fact at least partly that which lurked within the dualism of Locke is a historical point, but it does not affect the fatality through which nature becomes environed by the subject and the subject's sense-experience.

It was natural that Miller should have assigned one of Berkeley's *Three Dialogues between Hylas and Philonous* as well as Emerson in this part of the course. (In Philosophy 2, subjective idealism turned up once more in the assigned reading, this time as treated by Fichte in *The Vocation of Man* as a prolegomenon to the ethical idealism expounded in the last part of the book.) Berkeley is of course a perspicuous arguer; but, as I have already suggested, the arguments did not interest Miller nearly as much as the non-theoretical scenario for the discovery that nature has an environment.

In the Philosophy 1–2 syllabus, subjective idealism was followed by realism. In a moment, I will try to show the fatality that accounts for this transition. But first, a certain apparent confusion of the traditional divisions of philosophy needs to be cleared up.

Spiritualism and naturalism would normally be assigned to meta-physics; subjective idealism and realism to epistemology. Spir-itualism and naturalism are views of the nature of the real—of "what is in control," to use Miller's phrase—but with subjective idealism there arises a different concern. We can say "The agent is in control" or "Nature is in control," but the subject is not in control; he/she is a passive spectator of his/her own sense-experi-ence. What has happened is that views of *control* have given way to views of *knowledge*. In other words, metaphysics has itself been superseded by epistemology. Naturalism does not in itself pose a systematic problem of knowledge; it raises in itself no question about our ability in principle to formulate the laws of Nature. The problem of knowledge arises only after nature has been reformu-lated as the subject's construct from his/her sense-experience. For this experience guarantees no regularities, no laws. Consisting of nothing but a succession of sense-qualities, it perfectly exemplifies Miller's dictum that "Qualities tell no stories."[13]

Berkeley attempts to reconstruct nature within sense-experi-ence. It is to the regularities within experience that we give the names of natural objects and events and causal connections. But these regularities can never be necessary.

The move to realism occurs as sense-experience declares its own environment, i.e., the object. For it is only the existence of an object external to experience that guarantees the distinction be-tween knowledge and illusion; contingent regularities are never enough. Miller recited the arguments that led the realists to reject subjective idealism—"the shock of data," space and time as tran-scending mind, the world as common to all subjects—but it was clear that he did not regard the transition as occurring in response to arguments. Just as he could say "Subjectivism is a *resultant* of what we have studied so far,"[14] so he regarded realism as a *resultant* of subjectivism. There is a fatality in the transition. "The difference between reality and illusion is . . . *of the nature of thought*."[15]

It is important to understand that realism, as Miller taught it in Philosophy 1, is not simply a reversion to naturalism. It is epis-temology, not metaphysics. No doubt there are are many cases in which the distinction would be difficult to maintain. Amid the profusion of realisms that dotted the American philosophical landscape after 1900, for example, many of them had a natu-ralistic thrust. But one can still distinguish the naturalistic from the realistic vector of a complex position. It was naturalistic to assert the unenvironed status of nature. It was realistic to aver that nature presented itself as a possible object of our knowledge. It would never have occurred to a pre-subjectivist naturalist that it was necessary to make such a claim.

In view of all the versions of realism that were spun out after the turn of the century, it is tempting to think of realism as primarily theoretical in motivation. But Miller saw realism as thought, not theory. It was not an easy job to find texts to illustrate this point. (In at least one version of Philosophy 1, he used "The General Realistic Hypothesis" from the book *Personal Realism* by his predecessor at Williams, James Bissett Pratt.[16] But this is scarcely as important a document as The Book of Job [used to illustrate spiritualism], Lucretius [for naturalism], or Emerson or Berkeley.)

Realism claims that the object, or rather the world of objects or the objective world, is the environment of the subject. We must now ask whether there is a point of view from which the objective world has itself an environment—whether a fatality leads beyond realism. An answer to this question suggests itself in terms of the inaccessibility of the objective world.[17] That we live over against such a world is no more than a demand of our thought. We have no direct evidence of it.[18] We have no *evidence* of it at all. The object is an untrustworthy *illatum*. Descartes, whose *Meditations* were now used as a text, was not the first to count the ways in which the sources of our beliefs about the world are untrustworthy.

We have entered skepticism. Here the environment of the object is seen to be thought itself, since thought is the critic (or critique) that questions the general status of the object. Finding that we can no longer depend upon objectivities, we are confronted by the dreadful disclosure that *thought is responsible to itself and for itself.* We have come into the full estate of humanity.

Fell's notes at this point read "[Skepticism] can occur only within the 'fatalities of thought.'"[19] This is another way of saying that skepticism arises from no fact. It is not a response to an objective defeat. It can occur only when the thinker declares his *own* defeat—admits that he has committed an unavoidable error; confesses that he is systematically incompetent to know the object.

This was not the end of the course; we have now reached only the beginning of Philosophy 2. In the syllabus, skepticism is followed by "post-skeptical" positions, e.g., pragmatism, intuitionism, mysticism, existentialism, and objective idealism. But there is an ambiguity in the term "post-skeptical." Pragmatism, intuitionism, and mysticism succeed skepticism in the sense that they seek to retreat from it. Thus William James, perceiving that intellectualism can lead to skeptical consequences, offers an anti-intellectualistic alternative. This alternative is not a fatality of thought in the sense in which I have been using this phrase here; its motivation is more akin to that which earlier had given rise to dualism as an effort to sidestep the consequences of naturalism, preserving nature, but not as an absolute. We are not stuck with pragmatism in the way in which we are stuck with skepticism.

The other sense of "post-skeptical" designates a position that has gone *through* skepticism, rather than *around* it. Thus in his essay "The Larger Self," a further text in the course, Royce erects a positive position on the skeptical insight that the objective world is a demand of thought. This version of objective idealism was not, however, where Miller took his own stand. I leave it to my fellow authors in this issue of the *Bucknell Review* to clarify this point.[20]

It remains to examine whether there was really anything in common among the cases in which a transition from one position to another occurs as the result of passing *through* a fatality rather than *around* it. I have expressed these cases in terms of the concept of "environment," but they might have been expressed with equal felicitousness in terms of "limit," a near-synonym of "environment" in Miller's vocabulary. Thus nature limits the act, subjective experience limits nature, the object limits the subject, thought limits the object. We can see in each of these applications of limit a negative moment in the Hegelian dialectic. But I do not think that this dialectic is altogether mirrored in Miller's progression of types, since there appears to be no moment of synthesis arising from a typical operation of the fatality of thought. (Dualism as Miller conceived it is hardly a Hegelian synthesis, since it offers no genuine mediation.) Miller's emphasis, in other words, was not on a triadic form of dialectic.[21] Yet if one were to set out to learn what makes Hegelian dialectic tick, the progression of fatalities would certainly be a good place to start. I learned even without having set out to do so.

It might be possible to say a little more about the relation between Miller's dialectic and that of Hegel, but not a great deal more, because a certain looseness of both sides makes the concept of a dialectical transition somewhat ambiguous for both thinkers. While Miller tended, as I have tried to show, to regard the fated consequence of each type as having a position in a linear series or chain of types, it remains true that *if* he thought of his own notion of the midworld as a dialectical synthesis of subject and object, sublating the problem posed by dualism, then he was for the moment making use of a triadic dialectic along the standard Hegelian lines. But Hegel, for his part, was not always true to this standard, occasionally permitting a two-termed dialectical sequence to occur, and postponing or perhaps never even explicitly mentioning a synthesis. One example of a pair of dialectically linked terms for which no synthesis is immediately forthcoming is the Master-Slave pair in the *Phenomenology*—a pair that beautifully illustrates Miller's notion of the fatality of thought—"The Master declares his own environment." (Such deviations are perhaps more typical of the *Phenomenology* than of Hegel's later writings, where his commitment to triadicity became more explicit.)

So much for the concept of the fatality of thought as it figured in Philosophy 1–2. A question that could arise at this point was whether the fatality of thought was primarily a pedagogical device for Miller, or whether it played a systematic role in his own philosophical thinking. Part of the answer to this question is that nothing was ever a mere pedagogical device for Miller. None of his courses were to any great extent attempts to present material, and hence none depended on an ingenious pedagogy to facilitate the presentation of material. Miller played for keeps; he offered not material but the opportunity for self-revision. On these grounds alone, we can conclude that Miller must have been serious about the fatality of thought. But this is only part of the answer. In fact, what "lay in the cards" was the hinge on which all action, as Miller conceived it, swung; and action was the main category of his philosophy. Another article at least as long as this one would be required to develop this point on the basis of material in print and in the Williams College Archives. But one anecdotal consideration seems especially strong. Vincent Colapietro, who has approached Miller's work from a direction quite distinct from that of Philosophy 1–2, uses the words "fateful" and "fatalities" on several occasions in discussing Miller's thought.[22] Where could he have picked these words up except from the language of Miller's publications and nachlass?[23] They are words certain to catch our attention when used by or in connection with a thinker who was not by the wildest stretch of the imagination a fatalist.

Notes

1. This doubt comes through perhaps most clearly in Miller's recently published essay, "The Owl," ed. Robert S. Corrington, *The Transactions of the Charles S. Peirce Society* 24 (1988): 395–407.

2. William Ernest Hocking, *Types of Philosophy* (New York: Charles Scribner's Sons, 1929).

3. From notes by Robert E. Gahringer on Philosophy 1 as it was presented in 1947–48. These notes are to be found in the Miller Archives, Box 22, Folder 13. Later references to Gahringer refer to these notes.

4. A good set of examples of Miller's pejorative use of the adjective "ahistoric" is to be found throughout his essay "Afterword: The Ahistoric and the Historic," in José Ortega y Gasset, *History as a System and Other Essays toward a Philosophy of History* (New York: Norton, 1961), pp. 237–69. In this essay, Miller tends to identify the ahistoric with the Eleatic spirit in philosophy; see esp. pp. 255–56.

5. By "naturalism," Miller meant what many of us might be inclined to call "mechanistic materialism"; i.e., the belief that the nature of the real is constituted by matter in motion governed by deterministic laws. He did not mean the twentieth-century naturalism of Dewey or Buchler. That would have had another place in his sequence of Types.

6. On this point, see Vincent Colapietro, "Reason, Conflict, and Violence: John William Miller's Conception of Philosophy," *Transactions of the Charles S. Peirce Society* 25 (Spring 1989): 175–90.

7. Gahringer, 6 November 1947.

8. See Colapietro, "Reason, Conflict, and Violence."

9. Joseph Fell's notes for 4 December 1950 say that "[Dualism] goes back on Naturalism. It goes back on the very considerations that led to Naturalism." I take this to mean that Dualism does not constitute a transition from Naturalism to a position fated to supersede it.

Fell himself, however, in effect disagrees with my interpretation of his notes. In correspondence, he says:

> I interpet Miller's lectures as ascribing basic necessities to dualism: (1) in its origination or motivation, the necessity of jointly crediting the agent and the agent's critic (nature): (2) in its legacy, that from henceforth both the agent and its environment (both the subject and the object) must be recognized and must therefore be adequately interrelated (its positive legacy being the necessity of recognizing both free agent and nature; its negative legacy being its failure to understand the true relation between agent and nature). And the long and "fatal" shadow cast by dualism seems to me to be indicated by the fact that in Miller's view none of the successor-types of philosophy prior to historical idealism succeeds in resolving dualism's problematic legacy: how to interrelate (both ontologically and epistemologically) subject and object (i.e., only with the notion of the midworld is the negative aspect of the legacy of dualism overcome).

I resist this interpretation on several grounds. In the first place, dualism seems to me a juxtaposition of points of view, a deliberate attempt to have things both ways. Fatalities, however, are not deliberate. In Philosophy 1–2, Miller discussed several other deliberate occupations of positions, such as pragmatism, the intention of which is to evade skepticism; and I see no difference in principle between dualism and pragmatism on this score. In the second place, dualism arises from two sources, while in the sequences in which I see a strict fatality at work, it is the elaboration of a single source (e.g., spiritualism) that gives rise to its successor (e.g., naturalism). Finally, if mediation between agency and nature is sought, this mediation is worked out, just as Fell himself says, in the midworld (a concept not within the scope of the present article or of Philosophy 1–2), not in dualism per se.

But I am far from certain. What Miller himself thought about what he was teaching in Philosophy 1–2 sometimes surprised me. Consider, for example, the comment I made above to the effect that the succession of types in Philosophy 1–2 was an "ideal history." When my colleague Lawrence Beals and I once suggested this characterization to him, he stoutly declared that the history was not "ideal" at all. I am accordingly not really at all sure how Miller regarded the transition from spiritualism and naturalism to dualism vis-à-vis the fatalities exhibited in other transitions between types.

10. Fell, 6 November 1950.

11. Ibid., 9 April 1951.

12. Ralph Waldo Emerson, *Nature. A Facsimile of the First Edition,* with an introduction by Jaroslav Pelikan (Boston: Beacon Press, 1985), p. 63.

13. I had occasion to hear this dictum after Miller had been kind enough to read through a draft of my dissertation, "A Grammar of the Sense-Datum Language" (Harvard University, 1950).

14. Gahringer, 13 January 1948; my emphasis.

15. Ibid; emphasis in the notes.

16. James Bissett Pratt, *Personal Realism* (New York: Macmillan, 1937).

17. Miller often used the felicitous phrase "the epistemological gulf" to express this inaccessibility. Whether the phrase was his own, I do not know.

18. I here ignore the claims of direct and naive realism—technical theories that have not withstood the test of criticism. Miller mentioned them, but they obviously did not exemplify the type he had in mind when he spoke of realism.

19. 7 February 1951.

20. See in particular Robert S. Corrington, "Finite Idealism: The Midworld and Its History" in this volume. What Corrington calls "finite idealism" Miller himself often referred to as "historical idealism."

21. Vincent Colapietro reminds me that on this point Miller actually said, "Hegel, of course, had triads, but I think that the difficulty occurs as a pair. And while such a pair needs a third for its resolution, I prefer to see the third as the state of affairs that enforces the distinction." See Miller's *The Midworld of Symbols and Functioning Objects* (New York: Norton, 1982), p. 186.

22. See Colapietro, "Reason, Conflict, and Violence."

23. When I put this question to Colapietro one pair of examples to which he referred me was in Miller's *The Paradox of Cause and Other Essays* (New York: Norton, 1978), pp. 188, 191. I later came across a further example in "Afterword," p. 268.

I owe many thanks to Colapietro, as well as to Joseph Fell. The testimony of the former shows that a good historian can be more reliable than an eyewitness. That of the latter is a good illustration of how eyewitnesses can sometimes disagree, even if their testimony is by and large consistent.

Human Symbols as Functioning Objects:
A First Look at John William Miller's Contribution to Semiotics

Vincent M. Colapietro

Fordham University

I cannot get hold on a person *except* as I take him at his word. But does he speak? Has he spoken? Can *he* appear in utterance? ... If he speaks, in what way is he, the individual present in his word? What sort of word would that be?[1]

Indeed, what sort of utterance would that be? Can the world be conceived to include this sort of utterance? On the other side, what kind of world would one devoid of utterance be? Indeed, why should we persist in depicting the world as "silent," as a region in which neither speaker nor discourse has a place?

JOHN William Miller (1895–1978) was an American philosopher who exerted a tremendous personal influence on numerous students but, because he published very little during his career, made hardly any impact on professional philosophy during his own lifetime. In this, he was like many other academic philosophers. However, one important difference between Miller and so many other teachers who have also exemplified the Socratic life in an unforgettable way is that he fashioned a unique philosophical perspective worthy of the most serious consideration.

As we shall see, this perspective bears upon semiotics, though Miller himself would have been put off by much of what goes on today in the field of inquiry opened by Charles Sanders Peirce (1839–1914) and Ferdinand de Saussure (1857–1913).[2] Indeed, he would have been put off by the word itself and the very idea of a *science* of signs. Even so, what he offers, in effect, is at the very least a philosophy of symbolism.

Miller studied at Harvard, receiving his baccalaureate in 1916 and, after serving in the ambulance corps during World War I, his doctorate in 1922. Josiah Royce[3] and William Ernest Hocking were among his teachers. He taught for a very short while at Connecticut College for Women[4] and, immediately following this, at Williams College from 1924 until 1960, with one year interruption (when he taught at the University of Minnesota). From the year of his retirement to that of his death eighteen years later, he continued exploring a number of topics that had been the focus of concern during his years as a teacher. More often than not, this exploration was undertaken in conversation and letters.[5] These letters were often quite lengthy, occasionally over a hundred pages long. While Miller wrote countless pages both before and after his retirement, he published only several articles until near the very end of his life. In 1978, however, a volume of Miller's writings, *The Paradox of Cause and Other Essays,* appeared several months before his death. Four other volumes have been published posthumously. George P. Brockway, the editor of these volumes and a lifelong student of Bill Miller, has celebrated the career of his teacher in a memoir which appeared originally in the *American Scholar* and eventually in *Masters: Portraits of Great Teachers,* an anthology edited by Joseph Epstein. This anthology puts Miller in the company of (among others) Morris Raphael Cohen, Hannah Arendt, and Margaret Mead.

However, John William Miller was not only an outstanding teacher who exerted a lifelong influence on numerous students. He was also an original thinker who transformed objective "idealism" in an innovative way[6] and who made the semiotic turn at a time when it was not fashionable and in a way that is still challenging. "All knowledge," he claimed, "occurs through symbols" (*M,* p. 154). Thought no less than knowledge is symbolic; for even the "purest 'thought' requires a vehicle. It can be recognized only as it is incorporate. It is inseparable from that vehicle."[7]

Our world can no more be separated from symbols than can our thoughts. Miller refused to say, "There is the world, and here are the signs," as though our world could be severed from the media through which it is encountered and by which it is interpreted (*M,* p. 75). Apart from these media, there is no cosmos, only a chaos—no world, only a stream of private consciousness and a maelstrom of material particles, each internally anarchic and the two mysteriously juxtaposed. By virtue of these media (e.g., yardsticks, numbers, words), our modes of functioning (measuring, counting, speaking) become possible and, on the basis of these modes, our world is projected. "Leave out the Verbs [i.e., the modes of functioning] and there is neither Person nor

World" (MP 29:27). Insist upon the verbs and neither the cosmically situated agent nor the personally projected world is mysterious.

The world so projected is at once actual and precarious. It is dynamically both presupposed and proclaimed in the execution of our simplest acts and potentially threatened by any arrest of our functioning. The actuality of our world resides not in its absolute indifference to human purpose—i.e., not in its brute otherness—but in its intrinsic connection to human action. Our world is actual because it is projected, sustained and revised by our acts and also because our acts are always constrained and frequently frustrated by an inevitable antagonist, an inescapable other. Our world is precarious because this antagonist often proves to be too powerful for us.

Even the simplest forms of human functioning (e.g., the identification of an object) generate a dialectic of self and other—an ongoing, fateful process in which opposition and the drive to overcome opposition are central.[8] "The dialectic," Miller observed in one of his classes, "is something you know—it is right in front of you." It "is a very homely thing: it is near us, it is known to us, nothing remote." "Dialectic is the philosophical analogue of conflict."[9] Dialectic so conceived is no dance of bloodless abstractions but a confrontation of finite actualities. In this confrontation, the character of the world no less than the identity of the self are threatened by dissolution. As a result of such confrontations, the self *either* attains greater clarity and control *or* is overwhelmed by confusion and impotence.

Dialectical conflict needs an articulate vehicle (*PC*, p. 110), and it has this in what Miller calls "functioning objects." He observed: "It has been notoriously difficult to say how an error is possible in terms of mind or else of body" (*M*, p. 189)—especially in terms of a disembodied mind or a mindless body. But one finds "no difficulty in locating error apropos of the artifactual, in the yardstick in use, or in words. If one cannot find error in the pure object, neither can one in the pure subject. You have to *make* a mistake. It needs a venicle" (*M*, p. 189). If we turn to the midworld (the intersecting modes of functioning objects), such vehicles abound.

Functioning objects account for the possibility of not only simple *mis*-takes (e.g., taking this piece of wood to be four inches rather than three) but also dialectical conflicts. "We need to ally ourselves with the antagonist if experience is not to remain merely playful and subjective and so in the end, trivial and without dignity" (*PC*, p. 180). From the most basic modes of functioning (e.g., perceiving or walking) to the most complex (creating or interpreting a work of art), there is an active self and an *allied antagonist* engaged in a fateful struggle in which both self and other become simultaneously more sharply differentiated and more intimately connected. "Conflict does not operate to scatter the self but to establish it, even to organize it" (*M*, p. 187). The other over against the self is never an absolute other but always an allied antagonist—always a being in some way akin to the self and its commitments.

Nature in the distinctively modern sense is an example of such an antagonist. "Nature may be the 'Not-Me' (Emerson), but this 'Not-Me' is no present 'datum,' no magical apparition nor yet an absolutely alien region. Nature is a historical achievement" (*M*, p. 90). Nature as it is presently conceived is a region that came to be staked out by various individuals (e.g., Galileo, Newton, Einstein). "The region of nature as order is the implication of functioning objects" (*M*, p. 188). "Nature is then neither a perceived object nor an illusion but a fatal [fateful?] aspect of the original and self-declarative act. . . . The record is clear: divorce nature and functioning, and each becomes a dogma and a mystery" (*M*, p. 44). Nature appears to be so determinate in itself and so indifferent to us that "it seems folly to propose a midworld as its condition. But this is a systematic illusion. . . . The midworld, I believe, robs no one of nature. On the contrary, it is the means of saving nature from an arbitrary dominance, and of then preventing its inevitable dissolution in the acids of skepticism" (*PC*, p. 118).

Just as we cannot separate our world from the media by which it is made present and known, so too we cannot separate these media themselves from the modes of functioning made possible through these media. Put most simply, the yardstick is a *measuring* rod (a spatial measure) and, apart from it or something analogous to it, the measuring of space becomes impossible. A clock is also a measuring device (a temporal measure) and, apart from *it* or something analogous, the measuring of time becomes impossible. Both instruments enable us to discern limits, to mark boundaries. They do not facilitate a function already established; rather they themselves make possible in the first place certain ways of functioning, just as eyes and ears make possible distinctive forms of perception (perception itself being an important mode of functioning). Hence, yardsticks and clocks no less than eyes and ears are not facilitating but *functioning* objects, objects by which a type of function comes into being.

Miller's insistence upon the symbolic character of human

knowledge and upon the inseparable union of world and sign clearly indicates that his philosophical reflections took a semiotic turn. However, beyond this insistence, he proposed to explain human symbols as functioning objects and to conceive the totality of all such objects as the midworld of symbols. In his own words, the midworld is "utterance in all its modes, the locus and embodiment of control and of all constitutional distinctions and conflicts" (*M*, p. 7). It includes "yardsticks, clocks, balances, [numbers,] words, utterances, monuments" (*M*, p. 43) and numerous other functioning objects. Just as Saussure attempted to define the sign in terms of the arbitrary conjunction of signifier and signified, and just as Peirce endeavored to explain semiosis (or sign-activity) in terms of the irreducible triad of sign, object, and interpretant, Miller tried to explain the unique character of human symbols by means of functioning objects. In addition, just as Saussure and Peirce focused upon not a simple, isolated unit of meaning (the sign) but an inclusive, evolving network of signs, so Miller subsumed all utterances under the rubric of mid*world*.

Despite these proposals, Miller contended "there can be no absolutely general theory of signs" (*M*, p. 156). Hence, it might appear that his thought moves in opposite directions. On the one hand, Miller's thought drives in the direction of an explicitly semiotic account of self, world, and knowledge. Moreover, it does so in a novel way, since his most obvious and perhaps important contribution to semiotic theory is his innovative conception of a functioning object. On the other hand, Miller's distinctive conception of signs precludes the possibility of formulating a general theory of signs. Thus, we are in the presence of a thinker with a deep sensitivity to the semiotic character of "*our* world" and an equally deep skepticism regarding a general theory of signs. In other words, we are in the presence of a thinker from whom we are likely to learn much.

Miller desired, above all else, to do justice to the irreducible status of human utterance and to the *historical* dimension of all human endeavors. As we shall see, the only way to secure this status for utterance is to establish the categoreal status of historical process, to make a category of history (*PC*, p. 107). This entails taking history itself as irreducible and self-authenticating. The "price to be paid for enfranchising discourse" (*PC*, p. 107), for granting utterance the privilege to *tell* the difference between truth and error, reality and appearance, is accepting finite actuality as the sole locus of criticism and control. Miller's contributions to semiotics are intelligible only in reference to his endeavor to grant utterance and history their due.

To grant human utterance an irreducible status entails refusing all attempts to derive utterance from—or to reduce it to—something other than itself. Utterance ontologically either stands on its own feet or it does not stand at all—thereby collapsing into something other than itself. In fact, much discourse about discourse has been nothing less than an assault upon the status of discourse. (This is principally what inclines Miller to reject the possibility of formulating a general theory of signs.) For all attempts to make discourse something derivative, to derive it from a state of affairs in which both speech and speaker are absent (from what Miller occasionally calls either the "Silent World" or the "Voiceless World") amount to refusals to grant discourse any *actual* and authoritative status.

When Miller listened to his contemporaries (and he felt obliged to listen to even those who themselves refused to listen to others), he more often than not heard them saying in effect: The 'real' world is silent. It does not speak. Tales of the 'real' world are all illusion. They are 'myths,' i.e., stories. Abandon discourse all ye that enter here" (MP 25:22). In opposition to such contemporaries, Miller maintained that discourse must, *in general,* be taken on its own terms. It cannot be translated into other terms (e.g., physicalistic or behavioristic terms) without being transformed into another thing (a meaningless movement of material particles or an equally meaningless reaction of living automata). Without question, one word leads to another and often in this fateful[10] process earlier words are discredited by later ones, more primitive ways of speaking are replaced by more adequate ones. Accordingly, it is one thing to grant discourse, in general, an actual and authoritative status and quite another to grant this or that instance or mode of discourse the validity it purports to have.

Miller claimed persons, the utterances they make, and the world they inhabit are, when properly conceived, inseparable from one another (*M,* p. 70). An absolutely ineffable world is no world at all; it is indistinguishable from nothing. So, too, an absolutely mute self is no self at all; such a "person" is equivalent to no one. Stated positively, "communication is necessary to a self. To be a self is to communicate."[11]

Miller observed: "Some say, 'If the truth were told, talk is behavioristic and physiological and so, in the end, physical.' Here is an essay in telling the truth that needs no telling and has in the end nothing to do with telling" (*M*, p. 165).[12] However, this project is self-defeating: it inevitably *speaks* of a silent world in which both speech and speaker have no place. It talks of a world in which talk is impossible. Thus, in order to avoid this absurdity, what is required is showing how truth can be in the *act* of telling without being at the whim of the teller. Truth must be told[13] and it must be told by someone, some person, who appears as such in the very act of telling. For Miller, those who say "the truth is not in the telling" put themselves beyond criticism (*M*, p. 165). In contrast, those who insist truth is to be located in the act of telling (rather than some reality beyond discourse or some authority beyond criticism) do not merely subject themselves to criticism but, in this very insistence, establish the situation in which criticism becomes possible.

This point is as important as it is subtle. In one of his lectures, Miller claimed: "We must be alert to the conditions of our own discourse."[14] One task of philosophy is to deepen our awareness of these conditions. However, *our* discourse claims for itself the right to be critical of both ourselves and others. Whence comes this right? What makes critical (including self-critical) discourse possible? What renders criticism impossible? "The assumption of criticism is that we shall have a world of our own. . . . But what we have is then to be not only our own, but also a *world*" (*PC*, p. 118). A world is neither a total mess nor a finished totality. It is, to use an important word in Miller's philosophical lexicon,[15] *constitutionally* incomplete and, thus, subject to dissolution; but it is also constitutionally orderly and, hence, indicative of stability. Such a world is one in whose shape we have a hand and, as a consequence of this, one in whose destiny we have a stake. Of our world, Miller insisted "we do have a hand in it—the hand that picks up a yardstick, the tongue that tells time by the clock, the act that keeps tally by cutting notches in a stick or making a notation on paper, when alone the expression $7+5=12$ or $a+b=c$ becomes manifest" (*M*, pp. 108–9; original emphasis omitted). It is a world in which discourse is ineliminable. Accordingly, "there is no escaping an account of the sort of world that can include the utterances, the affirmations, and denials that permit any world to be intelligible" (*M*, p. 129).[16]

Miller stressed the historical character of our endeavors no less than the irreducible status of our discourse. "Our relations with time are," he asserted, "total and constitutive" (*PH*, p. 54). Even so, the recognition of this has been obstructed by the ahistoric temper of traditional thought (see, e.g., *PC*, p. 130). Miller, following the example of José Ortega y Gasset, called this ahistoric temper the Eleatic temper because it was in Elea "where there appeared a number of men who argued, with originality and brilliance, that change, and thus time, was an illusion and not reality."[17] This temper "finds the ideal of inquiry in permanence, in a substance or formula which remains [forever] fixed, which includes all change" (PH, p. 130) and perhaps even explains it. In particular, philosophy has been engaged in an attempt to escape from time. This is implied in its endeavor to see all time and existence *sub specie aeternitatis* (PH, p. 85).

History "has seldom *seemed* to be capable of satisfying our hopes, whether moral or intellectual" (PH, p. 130). Consequently, all the transactions of history "have *seemed* to require a point of view outside of time for their fulfillment and for their understanding" (PH, p. 130; emphasis added).[18] For Miller, this appearance is misleading. Our traditional mistrust of time must be overcome and a thoroughgoing alliance with time must be forged.

As we have seen, "action and the world are," for Miller, "inseparable" (M, p. 71). In general, act, actuality, acting, action are central words in his philosophical lexicon.[19] He himself noted: "While my interest was in the act, it was not primarily in science but in history. The status of history was insecure. It dealt in things done, in *res gestae*, not in things perceived. Epistemology, the theory of knowledge, had nothing to say about yesterdays. It proposed clock-time, not dated-time, invariance not genesis, the static not the revisory, the uniform not the unique. But it was plain enough that history rode on utterance" (M, p. 16). Hence, if the status of history is to be made secure, the *actuality* of utterance must be granted. "Make no claim to the here-and-now as authoritative, self-defining, and world-projecting, and dated-time [*historical* time] has no manifestation" (M, p. 110). That is, refuse to grant finite actuality an authoritative presence—stated more concretely, refuse to grant persons and their utterances the authority to define themselves and to project their own world—and history becomes impossible. Given such a refusal, history can be nothing more than a mechanical sequence of moments (clocked-time); it can never be a radical revision of outlooks (dated-time). In clocked-time, the difference between now and then, between the present and the other dimensions of time, is told without reference to persons and their deeds (though the telling itself is always the deed of persons). In dated-time, however, this difference is told either in terms unmistakably designating persons (e.g., "After Christ") or terms ultimately implicating persons ("post-modern").

History as the order in which radical revisions of ongoing endeavors occur is an order in which the difference between now and then is told in personal terms.

"It takes time to know the present" (*PH*, p. 112). The present is not known in an instant; nor is it known apart from the past. However, it takes conflict—the threat of dissolution—to want to know the past. First echoing and then extending an utterance of Abraham Lincoln (an act itself illustrating Miller's own contention that "all utterance prolongs what has already been said"), Miller claims: "We cannot escape history, and we cannot escape the study of history" (*PC*, p. 92). But there is not any history at all "apart from the thrust of present meanings into their yesterdays. History is a category because it is a necessary condition of the present (*PC*, p. 92). The study of history—reflection on the past—is an inevitable exigency of any confused present: "The past looms only in so far as the present is threatened with some disqualification, so that to understand itself as present it needs to undertake a story of its genesis" (*PH*, p. 115).

> History brings the past into the present, making it contemporary. The irrevocable past is not the historical past, but only the events and experiences which have served as the occasions and vehicles of a developing clarity. History is the implication of any self-conscious present. It is the mark of the realization that the present is not eternal but has been derived, and that its derivative status allows it to be identified as present. Without its past the present lacks distinction and peculiarity, suggesting no genesis and no further career. We do not study history because the past is a problem, but rather because the present is a problem. History identifies the present which, without history, is nothing but an arbitrary immediacy, without reason and without will. [MP 17:5]

The cultivation of an unflinchingly historical reason[20] is, thus, required for the maintenance of a constitutionally authoritative present.

While any actual present, insofar as it is a self-conscious present, sees itself as a "historical fate" (*PH*, p. 192), any historical fate in turn sees itself as an ineluctable affair of "entangling alliances" (MP 25:5) as well as "menacing mutability" (*PC*, p. 160). Such alliances are forged by means of a special class of human artifacts, namely, functioning objects. These objects are, in other words, the means by which we link ourselves with our past and, thereby, identify ourselves;[21] moreover, they are the means by which we thrust ourselves toward the future and, thereby, threaten any identity we have secured. Herein we see (at least, from Miller's perspective) the most important feature of human symbols.

As we have seen above, a functioning object is an incorporate actuality (*PC*, p. 125) "which embodies the verb—[for example,] organism, yardstick, clock, balance, number, word." These incorporate actualities are legislative as well as revelatory (*PC*, p. 128). That is, they establish limits (this is the legislative facet of functioning objects) and, within these limits, they create possibilities of encountering aspects of our world that otherwise could not put in an appearance (this is their revelatory facet). For example, space can *be made* to put in an appearance, but only if one brandishes a yardstick or some analogous object. Note that the functioning object is no ordinary object: "It proclaims other objects because it [itself] is more than an object. It is an object that defines other objects in terms of action and function" (*M*, p. 72). Objects in the ordinary sense (as the word itself says) are those things which throw themselves in our path (for example, the path of our sight). In contrast, functioning objects are the means by which trails are blazed in the first place (our eyes in the act of looking, *M*, p. 102). These are so far from objects in the ordinary sense that it is appropriate to question the propriety or adequacy of Miller's expression "functioning *objects*."

Be that as it may, what he calls functioning objects are not foci of attention but the loci of control. Without such loci, action is impossible. The endeavors to realize our purposes are possible only on the condition that we can expert control over both ourselves and certain features of our world. What Miller said of the yardstick is equally true of any other functioning object, namely, "it is tied to action, to doing" (*M*, p. 72). A functioning object also "leads to further action and to the experiences consequent on such action" (*M*, p. 74). "The present active participle [e.g., measuring, counting, speaking] has been overlooked by philosophers (*M*, p. 65).[22] Miller's concept of functioning object was designed to compensate for this unjustified neglect by philosophers.

While Miller acknowledged that much of what he said regarding the midworld and utterance sounds esoteric, he insisted that everything he proclaimed in his context "derives from *counting* my fingers and *going* to the post office" (*M*, p. 191) or from some other manner of functioning most properly identified in terms of a present active participle. Intellectuals have traditionally shown little or no respect for the various modes of incorporate functioning. Much talk of space, but none of yardsticks; much talk of time,

but none of clocks, etc. (*M*, p. 191). "Intellectuals [in effect] have
no verbs; the common man does." Because of this lack, Miller
declared: "I am joining that common man. And if this is a free
country, we'd better get ourselves a metaphysics that has respect
for the man on Elm Street" (*M*, p. 191).

Such a metaphysics rejects the absolute certitudes of the Cartesian *cogito* and embraces the menacing mutabilities of embodied
agents. In addition, it gives an unparalleled importance to the
human body and human artifacts. What is more, this metaphysics
sees the human organism itself as a functioning object. "The body
is," in Miller's own words, "*the absolute artifact,* that is, it is the
artifact that in its functioning creates all other artifacts and symbols" (*M*, p. 46). But it is by the creation of these other artifacts and
symbols that hominids long ago transformed themselves into humans and that humans ever after maintain themselves as such.
"The anthropologist does not come upon man until he discovers
the artifact, a revelation of *local control.* . . . Man is an artisan; he
makes artifacts. . . . The artifact is an awesome revelation. At
hazard—it is an incorporate psyche (*PC*, p. 125).[23]

It is in reference to artifacts that we come to know not only our
ancestors as human but also ourselves as actual. I come to know I
am (*sum*) through my actions. Hence, in a letter written late in his
life, Miller asserted: "As one may say, 'I rake, therefore I am,' my
amendment of Descartes. His world had no rake, nor any 'tool'"
(MP 22:14).

"For the man who handles a yardstick [or, for that matter, a
rake] thought is not unrestrained. For him it acquires a destiny
and a discipline" (MP 23:26). In general, human symbols (precisely because they are functioning objects) are the means whereby
our lives as well as our thoughts acquire a destiny and a discipline.
For Miller, this discipline drives us toward ever more refined
forms of self-legislation, while this destiny hurls us toward ever
more subtle forms of self-destruction. His account of symbols was
designed to exhibit the fateful power no less than the inherent
discipline of utterance (MP 25:22, p. 8).

He strove "to launch the word into the world which the word
articulates and manifests."[24] He endeavored to discredit the voiceless world implied in any number of influential positions. Put
positively, he credited our deeds and the world implied in our
deeds. He even confessed he heard voices, noting only madmen
hear voices. (It might be recalled that Socrates also claimed to hear
voices.) Yet, in the face of neglect and even ridicule,[25] he remained confident that the various attempts to grant authoritative

status to the voiceless world are what truly count as madness. The uttered world (the world launched by our utterances) is, when all is said and done, the actual world; and since *all* is never said and done—since there is always more that must be said and done—the actual world is a constitutionally incomplete region in whose shape we have a hand and in whose destiny we have a stake.

For Miller, utterance is not limited to discourse. Discourse is but one species of utterance. There are as many forms of human utterance as there are kinds of functioning objects, utterance being in this context the functioning object in its actual functioning or, more fully, the agent-in-act by means of such objects (the person, with yardstick in hand, taking the measure of a spatial area; or the historian, with monument in view, taking the measure of an ancient civilization). Symbols are only one species of functioning objects, and words are only one species of symbolic forms. Hence, discourse taken in the strict sense (i.e., utterance dependent on linguistic symbols) is far from the whole of utterance.

Yet, in utterance of any form, we encounter some person who is responsible for the utterance and, beyond this, the world launched by the act of utterance. Thus, "in the end there is the authority of some person" (MP 21:7) who vouches for the world, a fact recognized in such expressions as Homer's world or Plato's world, Darwin's world or Einstein's world. "The world is what *they* say" (*M*, p. 39). However, such authority "can't be established by a few words" (MP 21:7); it can only be established by countless words and other deeds. To repeat: "In the end, authority is in the person who *reveals* an environment" (*M*, p. 89). To be sure, few people assume such authority; "few speak words that are arresting in their clear disclosure of some commitment for which their author will stand, and if necessary go down in defeat" (*PC*, pp. 28–29). Most of us in one way or another evade accepting the radical responsibility of authoring *our* world. "But where there is grace and genuineness, one is under arrest"—i.e., one is arrested by the presence of an individual with the power to make utterances at once self-defining and world-projecting (*M*, p. 110). Such individuals are few. "But they are ones who live and who justify life and so they call the rest of us back to new courage" (*PC*, p. 28).

"Persons stir no emotion except as they are revelations, and this is the immediacy of the actual, of functioning, and of its manifestations" (*M*, p. 89). Persons who reveal a world do so through their utterances (e.g., Einstein through "$e = mc^2$"). Unquestionably, the individuals who make history are those whose words conjure up a world, a world which often bears their name. Miller explicitly recognized this fact about utterance; he even went so far as to assert: "Every word has some magic in it" (*M*, pp. 70, 75)—some power to conjure up something other than itself.[26] Indeed, every utterance is also a Pandora's box. Accordingly, there is not only a historical but also an enduring link between words and magic. In light of this, it seems plausible to suggest that the frequently oracular character of Miller's utterances[27] must be seen not as an idiosyncrasy of this speaker but as an ineliminable aspect of any unique utterance. How could *constitutional* discourse[28] sound anything but oracular?

Miller proclaimed: "I want the actual to shine and I want to feel the wonder of a yardstick, a poem, a word, a person" (*M*, pp. 191–92).[29] If this be madness, may all philosophers lapse into such lunacy.

Notes

This paper, in abridged form, was originally presented at the annual meeting of the Semiotic Society of America, University of Cincinnati, 29 October 1988.

1. J. W. Miller, *The Midworld of Symbols and Functioning Objects* (New York: Norton, 1982), p. 110. Hereafter, *M*, with page references cited in the text.

2. In his *Cours de linguistique générale*, trans. Wade Baskin (New York: McGraw-Hill, 1966), Saussure wrote: "*A science that studies the life of signs in society* is conceivable; it would be a part of social psychology and consequently of general psychology; I shall call it *semiology* [semiologie] (from the Greek *semeion* 'sign'). Semiology would show what constitutes signs, what laws govern them. Since the science does not yet exist, no one can say what it would be; but it has a right to existence, a place staked out in advance" (p. 16).

In an unpublished manuscript entitled "A Sketch of Logical Critic," Peirce posed this rhetorical question: "Would it not, at any rate, in the present state of science, be good scientific policy, for those who have both a talent and a passion for eliciting the truth about such matters to institute a cooperative coenoscopic attack upon the problems of the nature, properties and varieties of Signs, in the spirit of XXth century science [?]". The original copy of this manuscript is housed in the Houghton Library, the rare book and manuscript library at Harvard University. Richard S. Robin's *Annotated Catalogue of the Papers of Charles S. Peirce* (Amherst, Mass.: University of Massachusetts Press, 1967) provides a guide to the Charles S. Peirce Papers at Houghton Library. The draft of "A Sketch of Logical Critic" from which I am quoting is, using Robin's system of identification, MS 675 (p. 22).

He characteristically called this "attack" by the name of "semiotic" and described himself as a backwoodsman whose own investigations of "the essential nature and fundamental varieties of possible semiosis [or sign-action]" amounted to little more than opening and clearing a field of inquiry. *The Collected Papers of Charles Sanders Peirce*, ed. Charles Hartshorne and Paul Weiss, vol. 5 (Cambridge: Harvard University Press, 1934), par. 488.

In projecting the possibility of such an inquiry, Peirce (but not Saussure) was influenced by the concluding chapter of John Locke's *Essay Concerning Human Understanding* (New York: Dover, 1959) in which its author divides human knowledge into three branches—the "Knowledge of Things," the "Skill of Right," and the "Doctrine of Signs." Since the most useful of signs are words, this branch is aptly enough termed "Logick"—"the business whereof, is to consider the Nature of Signs, the Mind makes use of for the understanding of Things, or conveying its Knowledge to others" (2:461).

Miller was aware (though unequally) of the contributions of Peirce, Royce, and Morris to the study of signs. Moreover, a chapter of his own dissertation, "The Definition of the Thing" (Harvard University, 1922), was devoted to articulating what Miller himself would later consider impossible, namely, a general theory of signs. At the heart of his opposition to such an enterprise is the inevitable tendency to treat signs as though they were objects, language as though it were a datum—something found rather than joined, something constituted by a prior state of affairs rather than constitutional.

3. For a good introduction to Roycean semiotics, see Robert Corrington, "Josiah Royce and the Sign Community," in *Semiotics 1986*, ed. John Deely (Lanham, Md.: University Press of America, 1986). In volume 2 of *The Problem of Christianity* (New York: Macmillan, 1913), Josiah Royce himself writes: "Our experience, as it comes to us, is a realm of Signs" (p. 289). In an undergraduate paper entitled "Truth, Interpretation, and Reality" (25 January 1916), Miller echoed these words in this way: "The world of appearance is a world of signs" (p. 27). "Truth, Interpretation, and Reality" is to be found among the Miller Papers, Williams College Archives, Box 2, Folder 7. Hereafter I shall cite this source as follows: MP, followed first by box number and second by folder number within that box. John Deely in *Frontiers in Semiotics* (Bloomington: Indiana University Press, 1986) notes: "it is the realization that the whole of human experience, without exception, is an interpretive structure mediated and sustained by signs, that is at the heart of semiotics" (p. xi). It is precisely because I agree with Deely on this point that I think it is worthwhile to consider Miller's contribution to semiotics, for Miller fully realized that signs and symbols are among the most important conditions for the possibility of the distinctively human forms of experience and activity.

4. This institution is associated with another important but also neglected figure in semiotics, namely, Suzanne Langer, to whom Miller himself refers on several occasions.

5. Vincent Colapietro, "Reason, Conflict, and Violence: John William Miller's Conception of Philosophy," *Transactions of the Charles S. Peirce Society* (forthcoming).

6. "The idealism of the future will be a philosophy of history, of action, of a self-generating, lawful finitude." In J. W. Miller, *Paradox of Cause and Other Essays* (New York: Norton, 1978), p. 74. Hereafter, *PC*, with page references cited in the text. Thus, Miller occasionally spoke of his position as "historical idealism," an expression which signifies his continuity with the dialectical tradition of such thinkers as Fichte, Hegel, and Royce but which also suggests the novelty of his position.

7. MP 24:22.

8. In a letter to his son Paul Miller (1950?), JWM wrote: "in Hegel, the categories, as in Kant, are related to experience. But they also grow from experience. They do not grow from induction of particulars. They grow from another dimension of experience, namely its *struggle for coherence*. Experience in Kant had no dimension in time . . . In Hegel time is lived" (MP 21:8; emphasis added).

9. Joseph P. Fell's notes for Philosophy 7, Williams College, 6 December 1951; 13 December 1951; 4 December 1951. Hereafter cited as Fell.

10. See Henry W. Johnstone's essay "The Fatality of Thought" in this volume.

11. J. W. Miller, *In Defense of the Psychological* (New York: Norton, 1983), p. 170; emphasis in original is here omitted.

12. See Cushing Strout's essay "When the Truth Is in the Telling" in this volume.

13. J. W. Miller, *The Philosophy of History with Reflections and Aphorisms* (New York: Norton, 1981), pp. 152, 172. Hereafter, *PH*, with page references cited in the text.

14. Fell, 20 November 1951.

15. George P. Brockway, "John William Miller," *The American Scholar* 49 (1980): 160; Joseph P. Fell, "An American Original," *The American Scholar* 53 (Winter 1983–84): 128.

16. See J. W. Miller, "For Idealism," *The Journal of Speculative Philosophy* 1, no. 4 (1987): 268.

17. J. W. Miller, "Afterword: The Ahistoric and the Historic," in José Ortega y Gasset, *History as a System and Other Essays toward a Philosophy of History* (New York: Norton, 1961), p. 246.

18. While *theories* of history appear to bring "our relations with time" into focus, they actually amount to a denial of time. "When theories of history propose a general and supervisory view of all temporal transactions they suggest rather the other-worldly spectator than the finite participant in improvised deeds, adapted [or, better, allied] to time, suitable for maintaining a precarious present" (PC, p. 132). "Any 'explanation' of history is equivalent to the dissolution of a constitutionally authoritative present. It is the vanishment of the act in the alleged facts, of the agent in circumstances, or of all in an unordered 'stream of consciousness' " (*M*, p. 126)—or in an anarchical play of signifiers!

19. Brockway, "John William Miller," p. 238.

20. Ortega y Gasset, *History as a System*, p. 214; p. 223. Also see Strout's essay in this volume.

21. Miller, "Afterword," pp. 258–59.

22. See MP 24:22: "The intellect is either a baseless apriorist or else an anarchist [in other words, is either a dogmatist or a nihilist]. It looks for the 'meaning' of the Actual and fails to see the Actual [itself] as the source and warrant of any meaning. It has no legislative Verb, no incorporate and active present participle." See my "Conflict, Reason, and Violence."

23. For a compelling discussion of this particular point, see chapter 19, "The Portrait of Man," *In Defense of the Psychological*.

24. p.s. to a letter made available to me by Katherine Miller, Professor Miller's widow.

25. See Robert Gahringer's essay "On Interpreting J. W. Miller" in this volume.

26. See MP 24:22: "The primitive mind is 'primitive' because in its works and words it did not see itself but objects and faces other than a supposed person. Its works and words were reportorial, not revelatory. . . . The primitive mind did not see both itself and its World in its works and words. It had no Midworld in which both person and world were actualized and therefore both commanding and disciplinary. Magic was in things, in objects, not in the utterance itself. The idolatrous temper attributed magical influence to objects. We scoff at magic and in consequence allow no influential and determinative object, i.e., no local control. The role of magic has been taken over by the functioning object, never perceived but actual and not otherwise discovered. If the logic of Aristotle is to be influential it retains an element of the magical, but transfers control of person and world to the deed and the utterance. Eloquence is a magic, the incorporate vehicle of a person and world. Treat the word or other deed as a phenomenon and you deprive it of a revelatory power for both person and world."

27. See Strout's essay in this volume.

28. See Miller, *In Defense of the Psychological*, p. 162: "The business of the philosopher is to revise the constitution. Well, I propose some constitutional revision. That is not the same as proposing errors." It is much more basic and radical.

29. See Georg Wilhelm Friedrich Hegel, *Phenomenology of Mind*, trans. J. B. Baillie (New York: Harper & Row, 1967), p. 73. See MP 5:15 for notes revealing one of Miller's attempts to appropriate the basic insights from the preface to Hegel's *Phenomenology*.

Finite Idealism: The Midworld and Its History

Robert S. Corrington
The Pennsylvania State University

JOHN William Miller's conception of the midworld provides a metaphorical and categorial framework for redefining and strengthening idealism. Accepting the voluntarism of his teacher Josiah Royce, Miller struggled to find a proper locus for the realm of signs and symbols as they themselves illuminate the elusive features of nature and history. Unlike Royce, however, he rejected the sovereignty of pure consciousness and stressed the instrumental aspects of the emergence of the midworld. In what follows I explore several aspects of Miller's finite and historical idealism and raise some questions concerning the status it accords to nature.

In defining finite idealism it is important to distinguish between several possible understandings of the role of categories in generating and sustaining a portrayal of reality. On one understanding, categories can function as transcendentals that govern and locate all subaltern configurations in a necessary and universal conceptual array. Another conception of categories would stress their heuristic and inductive potency to render the precarious more stable for human apprehension and manipulation. On yet another interpretation, categories function as mere projective fictions that color and mask the deeper and more elusive traits that lie forever beyond human awareness. This third perspective is most commonly found in frameworks that embrace the so-called crisis of postmodernism. Miller's understanding of the role of categories does not fit into any of these more common models. Instead, he argues that the basic categories of philosophy are structures of criticism and derive their validation from practical and local control. In his 1938 essay, "For Idealism," he makes this clear:

> Categories are not transcendental, nor are they psychological or accidental. They are the structure of criticism, the dynamic of expanding meanings according to law. Thus, idealism asserts no Absolute, but

rather denies the possibility of any assertion immune from the order of contingency. It is that order which is absolute.[1]

The contingent events and structures of the world assume stability through the expansion and application of critical categories to more and more orders, as, for example, in the growing scope of the category of causality. Miller's idealism does not, however, mimic the instrumentalism of Dewey, which would have a seemingly similar view on the evolution of stability and meaning in instrumental control. Miller takes the claims and forces of history far more seriously than Dewey and sees the rise and spread of local control as part of the inner dynamism of history.

Dewey would deny that the environment is the human self writ large and insist instead that the momentary stabilities of the organism are the result of social and natural habit grooved into the fabric of nature. For Miller, the inner meaning of the environment can only be found through an analysis of the human will. In a letter written in 1949 he asserts:

> The environment is the self in its objective mode. The self does not assert itself, know itself, or maintain itself apart from it. Self-assertion in all its forms is also environment-assertion. Thus the environment is will.
>   It is "pure" will. It is the will in its generic form, not particular, but universal and essential.[2]

Where Dewey would limit the human will to problem solving and an occasional quest for qualitative integrity, Miller places the will right in the heart of the environment and insists that the self creates a realm of meaning that transcends bare instrumentalities.

Absolute idealism ignores the precarious and problematic qualities of the made environment and refuses to take novelty and contingency seriously. The finite human will, imposing form onto the contents of the environment, creates novel and spontaneous configurations. Such genuine novelties lie outside of the purview of absolute idealism. Miller contrasts his own perspective to that of Bradley and Royce, with particular reference to the status of the accidental:

> The pressure of this problem is evident in the type of solution which leading idealists like Royce and Bradley have proposed. At the last they present an absolute who is a "problem solver" with all the answers known, a mind no longer open to surprises, no longer confronted by its "other," no longer beset by that restless incompletion without which it fades into an inarticulate totality, without focus, and so without limitation. To the absolute mind all is immediately given, and even

time is metamorphosed into a "totum simul" where it ceases to have any of those features of form without which idealism is bankrupt.[3]

Form only emerges from the human will and its struggles to find an ordered but finite totality within the environment. The atemporal absolute has no limitation and hence no form. It cannot function in any meaningful way within or through the midworld of signs and symbols. Problem solving is the provenance of finite human minds rather than locatable within some alleged absolute beyond the ravages of time and the accidental.

Finite idealism rejects this ahistorical and detached Absolute of earlier idealisms and insists that all critical control serves the fitful but fairly determinate forces of history. Realism errs in underplaying the role of the human will in building the basic contour of the midworld. Skepticism, on the other hand, errs in denying the environment-constituting powers of the self and in encapsulating consciousness in its own "deluded" projections. Finite idealism stresses the power of form over that of content but not in such a way as to make all forms independent of their natural corollaries. The formal and the critical use of categories gives rise to an ordered finitude that has its own internal logic and that moves outward toward greater degrees of encompassment.

The concept of the midworld is logically connected to that of finite idealism. While absolute idealism would drive beyond the external world of mere description toward the atemporal realm of immediate appreciation, finite idealism insists that actuality lies somewhere between the finite subject and the environment that surrounds that subject. Pure appreciation is replaced by the critical and local use of instrumental categories. The power of the midworld is to some extent derived from its rootedness in history. This history lives on in the immediate present and fills that present with authority and a sense of necessity. In his 1960 "Afterword" to Ortega's *History as a System,* Miller argues:

> For now as in the past we call that our world which gives status and authority to the immediate. The record of these endeavors is history. There the modes of self-definition become explicit and serve as the vehicles for an understanding of what we have become.[4]

The midworld is the locus for the growth and movement of history. Insofar as the human process becomes open to the unfolding of history, it becomes aware of and permeable to the midworld that is the haven for history's self-presentation.

It is not sufficient to speak of the midworld as if it were merely a horizon of meaning that rides on the back of nature. The mid-world is constituted by signs and symbols that themselves derive their potency from functioning objects, some of which are concrete artifacts. History seems to concentrate its energy into the realm of immediate functioning objects. If we are to escape from the ahistorical we must return to the immediacy of the artifactual and reassert our local control over the present manifestations of the midworld. Miller, again in his "Afterword," makes this connection between history and artifacts clear:

> To a larger extent than we are aware we live through the past tense. The modes of this continuum are obvious enough, but they lack accredited status. We need a new epistemology, one that does not shrink from giving ontological status to artifacts. The past rides on them, and they are symbols and voices.[5]

Absolute idealism, at least in its Hegelian form, would seek for the past in the various shapes of self-consciousness as they unfold before the phenomenological observer who lives outside of the movement of those shapes. Finite idealism moves more fitfully and slowly through the concrete artifacts that live as embodiments of the midworld. Consequently it cannot gain a perspective outside of the midworld even if it can gain some sense of how the midworld has been shaped and expanded. Miller's position lies between Hegelian panlogism, which would gather up all shapes of self-consciousness into the dialectic of the categories, and historical skepticism which would see history as a realm without internal continuity. The midworld is not ahistorical but it does have its own dialectic, even if that dialectic will never produce a final consummation.[6]

Absolute idealism has been compelling in the history of philosophy because of a deep human fear of limitation and the constraints of finitude. Miller argues that our own reluctance to accept finite idealism comes from this existential failure to live within the actualities of the midworld. In his "Afterword," he links philosophy to this human attitude:

> The mistrust which philosophy has frequently encountered appears on the surface to be the consequence of extravagant conclusions: but its deeper source lies in the dislike, or even the dream, of maintaining the actuality of limitation. For that is self-consciousness and reflects its urgencies and responsibilities. A search for reality has also been a search for the self.[7]

Finite self-consciousness cannot escape from the ravages and responsibilities of history. The history of philosophy, while manifesting positive and progressive revision of the midworld, also represents a variety of strategies for ignoring the primacy of the midworld. The more positive conception of philosophy invoked by Miller would make the full meaning of finitude transparent to the self and at the same time provide practical mechanisms for transforming those conditions that do not support the deeper needs of the human process.

Philosophy needs to recapture the realms of immediacy from the flight that drives either toward a hard-edged and merely reactive 'realism' or toward the alleged comforts of the ahistorical. Using Hegel's arch metaphor of the owl of Minerva, Miller seeks to return to those daylight artifacts that give rise to culture and human history. If most of the history of philosophy is analogous to the nighttime flight of the owl, the philosophy of the midworld is the return to daytime presence and totality. In his essay from the 1960s "The Owl," Miller argues:

> The owl is a spectator, not a participant. He has no present. He looks for, and claims to find, a control within the spectacle. But this reverts to what is not local but all-embracing. On the positive side, there are reasons for owlishness: the failures to give the local an ontological status and to recognize in the functioning object the vehicle of all control and of all failure.[8]

The functioning object lives out of the heart of the midworld and derives its actuality from the powers of the human will as those powers work on the materially given. Miller's voluntarism again insists that no object is real that is not first the result of human manipulation and control. Unlike Fichte, who would envision an Absolute Ego as the source of the world-creating will, Miller insists that all acts of will come from the finite self in its drive to move outward from the local to the regional. Yet even in this drive for greater degrees of scope, the finite self does not attain an all-encompassing perspective. The functioning object serves as a constraint on the drive for encompassment.

Since we cannot appeal· to a global history or to some elusive "history of Being" (Seinsgeschichte) it becomes necessary to find and articulate specific environment-building acts. For Miller the past is the order of growth and manifests distinctive human purposes. History exhibits diversity and variety as the products of local control. "History deals with acts. Hence with purpose."[9] This purpose is not, of course, that of the absolute will that would move all finite actualities toward an ideal consummation or con-vergence. All finite human purposes are subject to endless revision and reconstruction as the realms of experienced immediate totality feel the pressure of the past.

History is the career of the will and can only be recaptured and appropriated through further acts of will. We clarify the various meanings of history through local control of those artifacts that seem to carry past acts of will. In a striking sense, the local artifact is the concretion of historical will and purpose. By placing his emphasis on the artifactual, Miller downplays the Roycean emphasis on an imperial self-consciousness that would swallow up all finite embodiments of itself.[10] The ofttimes fitful career of the past cannot be reduced to one infinite purpose any more than it can reveal a single set of meanings. Local control helps to reshape and redefine the very meanings and values that the past will have. Like Gadamer, Miller insists that the past can only become efficacious through specific interpretive acts in the present. These acts serve the larger purposes of local control and the generation of an environment of instrumentalities and meanings.

Finite idealism is historical idealism in that it limits the reach of the will to specific actualities that appear in the present as that present reactualizes the purposes of the past. Unlike Deweyian naturalism, which would replace the concept of will with that of habit, finite idealism places a fairly high priority on the importance of the human process as it imposes itself on the environment. The midworld, as the 'field' where finite idealism operates, is that side of the environment that is part and parcel of the human self in its quest for intelligibility and control. The midworld is precognitive in that it launches, spurs, and controls all cognition. "Unenvironed, it projects the environment."[11] Absolute idealism has the world in its entirety as its 'field' of operation. Finite idealism is correlated to the historical embodiments (incarnations) of the midworld. In a very real sense, finite idealism, with its legislation of form and partial totality, lives as the motor force for the growth of the midworld.

Human acts declare the environment. Miller's pervasive voluntarism seems to put undue emphasis on the manipulative side of the human process and thereby downplays or ignores the assimilative and reactive dimension of the self. Put in other terms, finite idealism sees the world as a made world and does not acknowledge all of the deeper senses in which the world gives itself to the finite self. In what remains I will explore this difficulty and indicate ways in which Miller's project needs internal modification.

Miller uses three technical terms that seem to operate separately: "nature," "environment," and "midworld." His overall perspective seems to privilege the concept of the midworld and understate the concept and reality of nature. The concept of the environment functions as a linking term between nature and the midworld, just as the concept of the midworld links the self and nature. In what follows I will concentrate on the concepts of nature and the midworld. There exists a tension between the voluntarism of local control and the sovereignty of nature. Is nature merely that upon which we exert control or does it have its own integral contours that impress themselves on the midworld? In some passages he seems to argue that nature does exert a kind of pressure on the processes of control. In an unpublished paper from 1949 he states:

> Nature always carries in its pocket a veto for any human act. When one says, then, that a natural condition is a factor in historical events, one means that history is impossible apart from the silent support of nature.[12]

Nature can veto any act that violates its own integrity and manifest this veto through its silent support of an alternative act. Nature in itself does not make utterances but helps us to choose between and among our utterances. It is unclear just how this support is manifest in any given case, but the validation structures seem to operate at a level 'beneath' the sum of all human acts.

Yet Miller also argues as if nature is without specificity until it becomes molded into the midworld. Nature is impersonal or prepersonal and lives as the form of finitude. In his "Afterword" he implies a kind of dialectical relation between the infinity of nature and the finitude of the self:

> Nature is not another object upon which we expend a bit of attention to the imprudent neglect of household chores or to the damage of higher purposes. Nature is the articulate objectification of finitude in its impersonal mode. The infinite is the form of finitude; and, conversely, the finite is the actuality of the infinite. Form is not fact, but function.[13]

In what respects can nature, qua the infinite, serve as the form of the finite given that Miller insists that true form is a product of finite acts of will? Is nature a kind of potential form that can only be actualized in the finite? If so, what constrains the way in which this unique pre-form becomes manifest? This passage seems to be in tension with his other statements concerning the mechanisms by and through which form becomes actualized in the midworld. Nature might be little more than bare possibility or, on a more dynamic conception, the realm of potencies that must become actualized through the midworld. Does nature need the midworld for its fullest expression? If so, this seems to make the midworld the inner telos of nature.

We can find some answers to these questions when we examine two other passages in Miller's writings that denude nature of anything formal or distinct. In this following passage, history is dramatically privileged over nature:

> History thus defines nature. Nature is both the cause and the limit of every unconditional resolve. Without history, nature remains a phantom, an appearance only, arbitrary and incoherent, a set of thoughts, without capacity to resist the will because not defined through the will.[14]

Here Miller sees nature as the spur toward those acts that move from the indeterminate to the determinate. His concept of definition is tied to his concept of the act. To define something or some complex is to carve it out from the vast matrix of nature and to locate it within the history of the midworld. If history defines nature, then history is the genus of which nature is the species. This startling inversion of the two realities places a great deal of pressure on the midworld as the actualization of nature's potencies.

Insofar as nature has an order, or, more specifically, exhibits innumerable integrities and orders, and it is not clear from the above how it can, such orders are manifest through the use of artifacts. In this second passage, Miller again privileges the artifactual and historical over the natural:

> Nature gives us infinite scope, yet even so, we must have telescopes properly housed, and apparatus to our hands that these hands have made. We must be equipped with artifacts if we are to discover the facts. Nature itself is not what we see and hear unaided. Its order, without which we do not identify it, is the order of these symbolic instruments, these functioning objects, which are the actual representatives of its structure.[15]

Nature seems to give us the 'space' within which to exert our artifactual control and historical reappropriation but is without any integrities of its own. Of course, facts emerge from local control, but the ontological realm of these facts remains ambiguous. Facts are certainly not antecedent to local control, this much is granted by Dewey, but they do not seem to have any standing outside of the signs and symbols of the midworld. Again we are compelled to ask about the specific ways in which nature exerts its "silent support."

If all form is finite then the concept of infinite form is a contradiction in terms. Nature cannot be a form of forms or a shape of shapes that somehow gives itself over to the midworld as an articulated sum of complexes and orders. The most that can be said, given Miller's overall conceptual structure, is that nature is a 'realm' of prearticulated possibilities or potencies. While there are many midworlds and many environments, there can be only one nature, even if it is difficult to render it into the categories of local control. Finite idealism, in spite of its obvious advantages over absolute idealism, remains one step away from the orders of nature that it struggles to serve. Of course, there is nothing wrong in talking of nature interpreted or of the world as an interpreted-world-for us. The question becomes that of establishing more clearly the senses in which our interpretive choices are intimately governed and compelled by the innumerable complexes of nature. The concept of the midworld is crucial to the inner logic of historical idealism, but it has become severed from the reality of nature.

I am not suggesting that we reject the basic insights and strategies of finite and historical idealism. What is required, however, is a larger metaphysical vista that will accommodate these insights without sacrificing the more basic and fundamental reality of nature. Finite idealism must be located within an ordinal naturalism that will show the precise ways in which the midworld is generated and sustained with the help of the innumerable orders of the world. This entails a de-emphasis on the powers of the human will and on the manipulative dimension of the human process. The self assimilates and endures the sheer otherness of nature and is grooved and molded by the traits that emerge from a realm beyond the sum of its willful acts.

Miller rightly wishes to rescue the accidental, the novel, and the spontaneous from the older idealisms of Bradley and Royce. His rejection of the absolute in favor of local control and functioning objects is certainly to be commended. Yet his consequent conceptual elaboration drastically narrows the scope of philosophy to the realm of culture and its history (Hegel's realm of "objective spirit"). More basic than will is that natural grace that comes to us from a spirit-filled nature. This grace cannot be experienced if nature is reduced to a kind of potential and preformal manifold. A kind of militant Kantianism blunts Miller's drive toward conceptual comprehensiveness. History is only one dimension of nature and is subaltern to other orders. Nature is that than which nothing greater can be envisioned. Consequently, the midworld is but one order within the innumerable orders of the world. While this order is unique and has its own novel array of traits, it is not sovereign. There are nonhistorical orders and orders forever beyond the reach of local control. Yet these orders are equally real and equally efficacious in defining the meaning and direction of the human process. The concept of the midworld, for all its metaphoric and conceptual fecundity, becomes omnivorous and attempts to totalize something that is at best regional and related to the inner dynamics of the human process.

Nature's support is not always "silent." The midworld doesn't exist in order to validate and define nature. The sheer survivability of any given midworld is determined by its inner acknowledgment of the articulate and demarcated orders of nature. The midworld lives in and through the grace of nature and serves that nature whenever it becomes permeable to the spirit that lives at the heart of nature. The midworld is certainly the 'place' where nature assumes human shape and utterance. But the power and richness of that utterance is only secured when the midworld opens itself to the sustaining orders within which it lives. Miller's eulogistic and heroic conception of the will must be chastened by the austere and life-giving potencies of nature. These potencies are not indefinite or bereft of form. They give the midworld its 'matter' and compel it to serve an articulated infinite that empowers all finite acts of will. Finite idealism is the perspective that analyzes and exhibits the outward face of nature. But it is not broad enough to encompass and exhibit the innumerable complexes of the world.

The midworld is only one gift of the spirit. If it becomes the place where nature itself appears, then it will serve the deeper needs of the human process. History is always nature's history. While local control can help to shape and embody this history, it remains embedded in the larger instrumentalities of nature. The birth, growth, and death of the midworld is one of nature's gifts. But this precarious gift points toward the heart of the nature that is the source of all grace. The midworld can best be seen as only one of nature's ejects and functions to enhance the plenitude of meaning in the universe. To confuse this product of nature with nature's sheer providingness is to efface one of the most fundamental distinctions of thought. On a deeper level, it represents a basic impiety against that primal ordinality which is the enabling condition for all orders.

Notes

1. J. W. Miller, "For Idealism," *The Journal of Speculative Philosophy, N.S.*, 1, no. 4 (1987): 267.

2. J. W. Miller to Edward Hoyt, 21 March 1949, p. 5; in Box 20, Folder 2, Miller Archives.

3. J. W. Miller, *The Paradox of Cause and Other Essays* (New York: Norton, 1978), pp. 42–43.

4. J. W. Miller, "Afterword: The Ahistoric and the Historic," in José Ortega y Gasset, *History as a System and other Essays toward a Philosophy of History* (New York: Norton, 1961), p. 241.

5. Ibid., pp. 261–62.

6. I owe this insight to my colleague Henry Johnstone, Jr., who refers to Miller's position as expressed in his Philosophy 1–2 course. See his essay in this volume.

7. Miller, "Afterword," p. 239.

8. J. W. Miller, "The Owl," *Transactions of the Charles S. Peirce Society* 24, no. 3 (1988): 403.

9. J. W. Miller, *The Philosophy of History with Reflections and Aphorisms* (New York: Norton, 1981), p. 32.

10. The relation between Miller's perspective and that of Royce is fairly complex. In a number of passages, Miller seems to be referring to Royce's pre-1912 metaphysics that articulated a more traditional view of the absolute as atemporal and ahistorical. Yet in other passages, Miller pays tribute to the semiotic and triadic understanding of the ideal interpreter in Royce's 1913 *The Problem of Christianity*. In this essay, I am concentrating on Miller's negative assessment of the so-called early and middle Royce (i.e., the Royce of 1885–1911). See Vincent Colapietro's essay in this volume.

11. J. W. Miller, *The Midworld of Symbols and Functioning Objects* (New York: Norton, 1982), p. 13.

12. J. W. Miller, unpublished paper, "The 'Cause' of an Historical Event," par. 21b; in Box 3, Folder 16, Miller Archives.

13. Miller, "Afterword," p. 248.

14. Miller, *The Philosophy of History*, p. 43.

15. Ibid., p. 148.

The Problem of Evil in Proto-Ethical Idealism: John William Miller's Ethics in Historical Context

Stephen Tyman

Southern Illinois University

IN the first introduction to his *Wissenschaftslehre,* Johann Gottlieb Fichte simplistically enough divided philosophy into the two basic camps of dogmatism and idealism, while further claiming that neither camp had the wherewithal "directly to refute" the other.[1] Far from constituting an irremedial loggerheads for philosophy, however, for Fichte this situation merely put in a proper light the true reason for preferring idealism. It is a matter of acknowledging the call and the integrity of free human action. This, admittedly, moves the question from what Fichte's mentor, Immanuel Kant, had so carefully marked out as the "theoretical" to the "practical" sphere. But it is the characteristic signature of Fichte's thought that concerns traditionally identified as practical (ethical) are moved to centerstage within the very strongholds of theory: "The world is the stuff of my duty rendered sensuous."[2]

Because Fichte broadly shared Kant's formal-categorical approach to ethics (now often called deontological), and thus found himself in possession of an a priori articulation of duty, it is appropriate to qualify his idealism as ethical in the full and proper sense of the term. Nevertheless, the factors rendering apt the title of ethical idealist were not intended to diminish the ontological (theoretical) dimensions of Fichte's effort. Whether the reliance upon the sense of duty does not after all introduce at least the suggestion of practical elements into the heart of an ontological idealism that would, to be true to itself, remain more pure, is a question that remains vexed. In any event there is no doubt that Fichte was aware of theoretical considerations favoring idealism even if not definitively refuting its opposite: "[Idealism], indeed, has this advantage over [dogmatism], that it is able to exhibit the presence in consciousness of the freely acting intellect."[3] With this, at once the foreshadowing of the self-referential dimension of all theoretical phenomenology and a compact rendering of Fichte's tilt toward ethics, the leitmotif of idealism is established as the free act. Could it be a mark of Fichte's genius rather than an eccentricity that one searches in vain in his thought for a sense of the ontological that is not already on the way to the ethical? But does being on the way to the ethical necessarily mean a raising of what ought to be above what is? If not, may we then perhaps think these two dimensions of the ethical and the ontological, the practical and the theoretical, in their primordial togetherness as determinative of an idealism which is "proto-ethical?" It is in this connection that I would like to introduce the ethical thinking of John William Miller.

It is the thesis of this paper that the problems and themes of proto-ethical idealism, all too easily neglected by a humanity infinitely resourceful in concocting ever new dogmatisms, have been taken up again by Miller. By putting the matter in this light, I hope partly to supply the context that animates a philosophy a good deal of which has been published posthumously as much as half a century after its composition, and partly to propound the positive theme. The direct issue, I say, devolves around the access of self to self in the free act. Idealism here is the claim that this self-access is not only possible but can be taken as philosophically foundational. We do need to recognize, however, that opponents of idealism have always claimed that it provides too much intelligibility, more than can be squared with experience. It is customary, then, to oppose some inscrutability, some darksome factor, to the idealist's claim when this is what is to be refuted. Often this is done with reference to the putative "givenness" of the world or what is in it. But this thrust is parried by the shift from a strictly theoretical to an equally primary practical idealism: to be is not to be perceived but to belong to a problematic of the often dark and ambiguous give and take of engaged *doing*. It is a question of the integrity of act, not the prevalence of light. The complaint, however, may then change focus, alighting upon the question of negativity and inscrutability in the sphere of practical action. The issue now becomes recognizable as the opposite of proto-ethical action, the problem of positive evil. This is the fundamental question for explication and defense of the proto-ethical idealism of John William Miller.

Let me begin with the caution that in approaching the question of ethics in Miller's unique idealism one must be prepared to yield all expectations associated with ethical programs aimed at deriving from some theoretical basis specific recommendations for human behavior. We can find in Miller's writings little or no contribution to positive morality. Nor is this an accidental omission. For Miller's view is that so much of behavior is valuable and intelligible only in relation to the historical and cultural conditions which motivate and contextualize it that no formalization of behavioral rules can lay claim to universality. But this is not to say that Miller is a relativist, or that he is unconcerned with morality. His reflection in this area attempts to cut through to a deeper stratum, to seek a basis in the human condition.

Now for Miller, no means of reflecting upon the human condition can lay claim to what is essential, let alone be comprehensive, so long as it fails to get to the root of action. For to understand what human beings are is to understand what they can do, while to understand what they can do is to grasp their most intimate and revealing freedom. To say that freedom of action lies at the core of human existence admittedly risks cliché and vacuity; but in a positive sense, it also puts at risk an overweening tendency to relate to the human condition in factual, objective, and psychological terms. At the outset, then, we distinguish between the affirmative aspect of Miller's claim, which does show what I will call compactness, and the negative or critical aspect, which relates to the many means devised by positive science of understanding human action through phenomena alone.

It would appear that the tendency to behaviorism in psychology, an attempt to imitate "hard" science, but which only skips over the essential point in human action, is grounded precisely in the compactness of freedom. Freedom, pure and simple, is imponderable through description or reconstruction, particularly if these proceed in such a way as to take it as something given, extant. Freedom is so elusive as always to slip through the fingers, so to speak, of those who would hold it in their grasp. Of course this insight is not unique to Miller, even if he looms now as potentially its most compelling proponent.

Miller thinks the act that merits the name of freedom is self-originary in the same decisive sense that Kant did: it is not the product of a *quality* called freedom, but its living embodiment, its self-assertion. This means it is not to be understood as the pursuit of goals given through the framework of antecedent desire, which would in that case specify it as passive in relation to an extrinsic "nature." All specification here is self-specification. That means that the natural disposition, together with its valuational framework, is itself a product of freedom. The matter is handled in the

Kantian idiom by saying that the act is noumenal rather than phenomenal; freedom, expressive of the intelligibility of the self *in itself*, is yet not intelligible *to us*. Thus for essentially Kantian reasons the act-character of actions can no more be got at via their phenomenal description than can their possibility as free enactments be demonstrated by reference to phenomenal proofs.[4]

Now with regard to the question of the character and possibility of actions as actions (actions as free), everything depends upon what Kant called the legislative function of pure reason, which for him is equivalent to will. The moral character of an act depends not upon the (phenomenal) laws of nature, but upon the freely self-given laws of an agency with which in the highest sense the self is to be identified. For Kant, however, this fundamental movement of moral action may be thematized only against the backdrop of the dark side of the problematic, the natural humanity subject to the universal reign and sway of natural law. That Kant's efforts to establish the viability of freedom so fundamentally depended upon this distinction is testimony to the extent of the concession he actually made to the determinism of the day: the determinists are already well in possession of the penumbra or ghost of human action before Kant attempts his limited exorcism in the moral domain.

The important point here is that Kant's way of championing the cause of morality represents a retrenchment within a kind of hypothetical and reconstructive formalism in relation to the motivational background of action that has lost altogether the fluid, self-referential element of desire. Utterly gone, for example, and sacrificed to the exigency of the defense against the specter of the automaton self, is any possibility of the happy harmony of the classical (Platonic) humanity in whom the erotic and the rational-moral impulse are one.

From this split between the natural and moral self stems the great anomaly of Kantian ethics, expressed in his unique problematic of motive. For Kant only the higher (nonnatural) self is genuinely intelligible (noumenal) as a self.[5] It is so embedded in its legislating function that it is recognizable only in relation to how it stands with regard to its chief effect: the moral law. This is the price of Kantian freedom: either an act is done for the sake of the moral law which it effectively co-enacts, or else it is lost in the self-oblivion which Kant associates with desire. Desire, so understood, is part of a natural phenomenality that carries laws of its own, leaving no room for the (free) act-character of a human act. Free acts are defined in opposition to this, as acts that carve out their own unique intelligibility by inscribing the moral law within themselves. This gives rise to the dilemma, however, that no free acts can be less than moral. With this, the negative side of the moral situation becomes unthinkable, and likewise, any possible exhortation to morality making appeal to a common motivational life.

But at a deeper level this anomaly is only a further consequence of the *kind* of compactness with which Kant thought the identity of practical reason and will.[6] This said, one can yet see what Kant had in mind: it is this identification which enabled him simultaneously to attribute a constitutional structure, once and for all, to free will, and to find in the consequent application of the self-engendered law, the body of practical results he generated from his rational criterion of self-consistency, the categorical imperative. This arrangement does justice to Kant's deepest insight into the wellsprings of freedom, which retains a measure of inscrutability even while allowing the assertion of a bridge from theoretical insight to practical consequence.

Here, however, there is an irony: while this maneuver of deriving the particular conclusion from the universal criterion was necessary to give Kant the result he wanted (a workable ethics), it was effected in such a way as to reify, and thus devitalize, the very relation which most animated him. It is the relation between what an act establishes as its constitutional structure and the context in which it comes into play. Just because of his uncontested capitulation of the field of desire and the consequent split between freedom and nature, Kant could allow no motivational interplay between constitutional and contextual factors. The theory-practice split permits a deductive projection from the former to the latter, but not vice versa. Here is Miller's question: Does not ethics live only in this interplay, this reciprocity?

If we put this point together with the earlier one about the problem that no free action can be immoral, we have the basis of an approach to Miller's departure from Kant. We must admit, however, that, in his practical lectures, at least, Kant seems unconstrained by the rigidity of his own theory, as his ethical counsel there, however peculiar in some respects it may appear, still does not seem to be the blind application of principles, and surely the impulses of nature are given their due. However, in *Religion within the Bounds of Reason Alone*[7] where Kant's recognition of the positivity of evil precipitates a revision of the other implication, that moral and free action are coeval, Kant studiously avoids any softening of the division between the inner resource of freedom and the exterior provenance of desire. That the freedom/nature rift falls thus within the person still bothers him not at all, since it is only the person taken as active constitutor of the law, not as subject to the passions, that Kant wishes to preserve as free. Instead, the newly admitted radical character of evil for Kant forces the recognition of a second basis of self-constitution in a moral sense: evil is set over against good as an equally basic possibility for the will.

In this new sense the legislative factor, still that which produces the moral law within, can no longer be the immediate consequence and embodiment of freedom, but comes to occupy a position of ambiguous primordiality in relation to a will whose self-assertion retains a problematic reference to the imperative it can now defy. For its part, the will comes to admit a duality at its source, and its identification with the unifying factor of reason is harder to sustain. This latter point becomes a major topic of exploration for the post-Kantians. In Schopenhauer and Nietzsche, however, and somewhat less emphatically in Fichte and Schelling, the priority is reversed: in this suggestive union between will and reason, more of the elements traditionally associated with willing than with reasoning are to be found.[8]

It begins to seem that precisely those factors of Kant's analysis of the moral situation that most strengthened his hand against determinism are decisively eroded by his admission of the positivity of evil. The principal loss is to the conception of the autonomy-transcendence nexus for which he originally argued, always in the hypothetical mode, as the deductive consequence of the presumption of human freedom. The point is simply this: if, in the first instance, the morality one discovers is a metaphysical entailment of a certain conceptually circumscribed version of individual freedom, one is hard pressed to retain the former while expanding the latter.

The problem of evil continued to haunt the post-Kantian idealists, at least to the extent of provoking Schelling, the leading figure of the movement in his time, to offer later in his career and once again in the context of the thematics of freedom a revised system that raises the source of negativity or evil to cosmological status alongside the primordial source of positivity, the good.[9] But Schelling belonged with Hegel and (to a lesser extent) Fichte and their later British and American admirers in having abandoned the problem of constitutivity that Kant approached in terms of the formula "the condition for the possibility of. . . ." In its place were substituted various combinations of alternatives ranging from his-

torical to speculative-ontological factors, often dialectically considered, that played a mediating role, breaking up the "spurious"
necessity of Kant's a priori, and at the same time eliminating what
I call its "compactness." This variation that for Kant would have
been such a great loss, but for his followers was deemed such a
gain, constitutes the nub of an array of issues whose oblique
relation to our present concern is enough to suggest separate
treatment. Miller's way of handling these themes does prove revealing, particularly in view of his continued allegiance to Kant in
respecting the unmediatable compactness of the constitutive dimension. What this means, in effect, is that Miller is wary of "too
much" intelligibility: he prefers the mode of critique to that of
speculation.

So, to return to the point of Miller's relation to the Kantian
analysis of morality, we find as the root of his disagreement not so
much the emptiness or formalism of it, but rather an alternative
view of desire and evil. Of course the chief question here is the
extent to which one can effect this departure while remaining true
to the conception of the self-generating moral law, whether or not
this latter becomes expressed in Miller's preferred terms of form-
engendering act. The whole problematic is rife with consequences
running well beyond the standard moral range.

Consider first Miller's reconstructed version of desire. The
problem is to rethink the role of desire as integrated into the
economy of a being essentially free through and through. But if
this is thinkable, desire can no longer be merely immediate nor
finally compulsive. Desire is not a bit of external nature lodged
indissolubly in the dynamics of action. Nature, if it comes into play
in the psychology of primal urges, must be liberated. But for
Miller this does not mean that we are left with the giddy euphoria
of an utterly innocent or purely ecstatic desire. Where all yearn-
ing, even down to the most degrading clutching and grasping, or,
worse, the blind and perverse urge to dominate and desecrate, is
morally neutral, morality as a genuine life-task is obliterated.
Morality survives only in the tension of a constitutional indeterminacy holding sway between, on the one hand, a desire which is
neither self-regulating, self-sustaining nor able to gain hegemony
in motivational life and, on the other hand, an overriding super-
ogatory critical-rational function which can hardly be delineated
or observed except in relation to that conative life for which a
context-bound self-control is an issue.

Thus, the decisive point in relation to desire is twofold. First, it
does not form a closed system: desire of itself already reaches out

to what complements and completes it. This means that the coupling of desire with a moral factor is not extrinsic but intrinsic, not adventitious but necessary, arising from within the telos of desire itself. As Miller prefers to say, the moral dimension enjoys a constitutive status in relation to the act of desiring. Second, however, there is not a complete homogeneity of desire and the governing factor, whether this be called will or reason. A self-critical function is still opposite to what is desired. This is why moral conflict is possible, or, put more strongly, why conflict is germane to the context of morality. Desire is not static, but, because it longs for a completeness it could not countenance if it were found, reveals a lack of homogeneity even within itself. It is within this constitutive lacuna that the distancing function of rationality, again with constitutive status, arises within desire. Thrown back upon itself in opposition to the critical moment arising within it, desire could be merely the embodiment of unrest, a constitutional contradiction, a self-contracting ecstasis that, in its dizzying freedom longs to be controlled, while in its moments of greatest constriction longs again for its purer and unspent form—its freedom. Most particularly in relation to the problem of its self-governance, then, desire presents a paradoxical figure.

This state of affairs can be projected back upon the question of freedom versus necessity within the heart of desire. Miller writes: "In general problems cease to exist where desire needs no governance. This is the state of affairs where (a) any specific desire is avoided . . . (b) all desires are avoided (death) . . . (c) all desires are fulfilled, as in intoxication or fantasy. If the ethical problem can be avoided by such extreme measures, it follows that it can be accepted only with consent. Yet a problem to which one consents seems not necessary, because avoidable. Thus ethics suggests a paradox: that its problem is both unavoidable and freely accepted."[10]

This gives the setting of a structure to which Miller returns again and again in his effort to view the central motif of free self-grounding action in an ethical context. What must be understood first and foremost is the very strong call to freedom embodied in Miller's founding insight, and that this freedom functions constitutively in the project of conceiving a formal framework of ethical action. This first insight can enter into its full intelligibility and its formal and constitutional status only when it is realized in a nonarbitrary, that is to say, a necessary, way. Thus: "There will be no necessary answers (duties, rights, etc.) where there is no necessary problem."[11] But the necessity of the problem can arise only from the exigencies of a radical freedom at play within conative life.

Here we face a basic transformation of the Kantian call to ethics. For Kant morality is the inner telos of a freedom that establishes itself as transcendent to desire. Miller's position is that freedom loses none of its radical character, but rather first regains its own reality, when it is instead recognized in the very substance of desire. But Kant, nevertheless, was right in his equally basic insight that it is desire that is overcome in the transcending movement of freedom. The conclusion to which we are led, then, is that it is desire which, to fulfill self-imposed demands, must overcome itself.

Now desire, entailing in a profound sense a proclivity for worldliness and engagement, can never achieve this as the direct application of a general rule drawn "from above." It rather generates a transcendence within itself, in a kind of self-fracture, a violence turning inward. From this process, dynamic, engaged, and contextual, a value emerges as something highly particular, witnessed not simply as desired but desirable. For Miller, living value is context-specific. No transcendental account could render an objective norm from the a priori analytics of desire. On the other hand, our ability to think the constitutive factors in moral life is another matter. Here no particular value is in question, nor is the context that calls for it. Instead it is the form which becomes the content. The relevant cognition remains merely formal insofar as it appertains strictly to the free structure of complementarity and dehiscence of self-governance and desire.

Note that no special epistemological derivation, no transcendental deduction, is involved. Miller's method is critical, phenomenological, and metaphysical at once. But all three terms must be seen in the context which his philosophical activity uniquely provides. The overall character of his thinking is phenomenological in the sense that it contains the characteristic moment of the reduction, which effects a shift of attention to the essential active and constitutive factors in experience, away from the first-order contents. But he could also be called metaphysical-critical in the sense that he understands his formulations not to be descriptive of a specific stratum of the constitution of experience, but a compact yet correctable reflection upon the formal structure co-enacted within everyday experiential activity. The generality of the enterprise is as undeniable as the fact that, in its general way, the cause it most emphatically champions is that of specificity.

When Miller declares for the all-embracing freedom of the will, then, he is well aware of the surplus of the meaning over and above the more limited case of an individual act of choosing. Seen critico-phenomenologically, the individual act is a representative of the general factor. For philosophical reflection on the form of the moral condition, this move is essential. But it would be disastrous subsequently to reapply this mode of analysis back to the account of an actual case of moral action. One does not actually expend one's freedom at the general level. One does not will anything like the good itself, nor can we regard the specific good as a case in point or an interpretation of a purpose abstractly held.

Purpose, instead, is part and parcel of the circumstances which necessitate making a choice. Motive belongs, too, to the content, and is subject to the same exigencies of variation and amendment as a project unfolds. Rather than to identify an essentially abstract rationality with a putatively pure will, then, Miller insists upon a rationality committed to purposeful action yet undominated by preestablished purpose. Thus: "Only if the purpose that suggests choice is itself tentative can the choice be rational. For an absolute purpose the choices of execution or fulfillment are equally absolute. That is to say, choice, as a selection of alternatives, is irrelevant to an absolute purpose."[12]

With this analysis of the role of motive in (free) action, Miller embraces the realm of purposes as a second variable, and accordingly a second defining dimension, whose primordiality in specifying the character and implication of moral action is equal to that of the available means. He does not think in terms of an essentially good will being cast in the position of needing to secure for itself the means and focus for its enactment, or applying a formula for good behavior concocted merely from its own resources. While ends and means do not comprise a continuum, in their discontinuity they provide a reciprocity and tension that opens up the moral dimension. It is only a determinate framework of action, ethically articulated by a unique collision of ends and means, that tends to the good or the evil.

Meanwhile, since all purposes exist in a state of reciprocity with the conditions in which they are launched, they always remain subject to revision. The good one has in mind can and often must be altered, but this does not impute to one a diminution of good intentions. The commitment remains, though it cannot be identified and dealt with except in relation to what it is committed to. In sum, "In ordinary choice, the activity proposed in the choice may lead to a revision or even removal of the launching purpose . . .

But, assuming it made sense to set about doing good, nobody suggests that in doing good we may find the game not worth the candle. Nobody, that is, except the amoralist."[13]

In this way Miller thinks to have taken a major step toward dissolving the great dilemma of ontological ethics, the problem of evil. Instead of, in the later Kantian fashion, discovering in evil a motivational sourcepoint over and against the good will, yielding a duality in the dynamics of willing, Miller finds but a single nisus, and this to the good. The psyche is teleologically inclined to the fullness of being, to the perpetuation of the conditions of self-enactment. So the question is how activity of itself, unmediated by other psychic or ontological factors, can be conceived as capable of evil, yet possessed of an inner disposition to the good. The clue resides in the plasticity of the factor of self-identity, which is uniquely self-establishing within every specific act, yet carries with it an ontological "surplus": the self creates itself finitely through its own action, but in such a way that, in a constitutive manner, it retains a sense of its own incompleteness. This is equivalent to the retention of a sense of self as potential, as ongoing project. While this adumbrated selfhood cannot yet be characterized in determinate terms, it still constitutes a source of value, namely that of the continuity of its own life. Thus the nisus intrinsic to free action, and the manner in which the good is to be located within the dynamic conditions of human behavior, belongs to the persisting desideratum of self-maintenance. By contrast, the mischance of evil lurks in the possibility that actions can be effected in such a way as to close off one's most vital opportunities by flying in the face of actual, finite, life-giving circumstances. To the general point, Miller writes: "The moral is the maintenance of rational choice, that is, of conditional ends, and so of conditional means, where both ends and means are determinate and specific. The non-moral is the loss of such activities . . . The immoral is the treatment of a possibility without reference to the finite actuality which gives one identity and limitation."[14]

With this remark, Miller edges, still within his own ambit, toward one telling element of the Kantian view: the tendency to regard moral failing as a self-contradiction for an essentially transcendent being. But for Kant originally this result was tied to the earlier motif of the identification of will with the problematic of "pure reason in its practical employment"; with the later move toward an independent bivalent conception of will (motivated by the question of evil), the theme was dissipated considerably. Now Miller's own inclination is to remain closer to the defensible core of the earlier view. For him this entails not so much the value-formula for achieving moral action expressed in the categorical imperative, as the value of keeping open the possibility of acting, in his strong sense of the word.

Here the role of the consistency-criterion indeed permits the identification of the rational and the moral, but while both considered as abstract criteria are formal constituents of moral life, neither can be milked to achieve consequences or formulas for action. Suddenly Miller's sense of practical rationality begins to show more affinity for the *Nicomachean Ethics* than for the *Critique of Practical Reason*. The role of practical rationality is to seek direction within the nonrational dimensions more than to dictate the law.[15] Miller's view of the legitimate role of reason within an essentially affective and situated moral life, then, is that it functions in such a way as to support the continuity of precisely those projects through which this life derives its meaning, worth, and effectiveness. This is accomplished as much by addressing as they come up the never-ending stream of unforeseen exigencies as by busying itself with the best-laid plans. A failure to master actualities is a failure in the nerve of rationality and morality at once.

Miller's position, then, with regard to failed morality, sin, or evil is that at bottom what it represents is a failure to respond effectively to the conditions requiring action for the maintenance of value in life. What gives these conditions the intimacy and urgency essential to the moral situation is not the formal requirement that the action be undertaken, nor again the mere concrete possibility of the action, but the fact that the action itself looms as an essential part of a meaning-generating commitment. Miller writes, "Every specific act emerges from a matrix of commitment, a commitment necessary in principle but accidental in its content."[16] When an action goes against the grain of the prevailing commitment, then, it establishes a contradiction within the sense of meaningfulness and renders the life lived in its service, and indeed the very life which gives meaning to the action itself, less than whole. The contradiction involved in an immoral action, then, is an existential more than a conceptual one.

But can such a thing be done on purpose? Is radical evil thinkable in these terms? Miller himself shows some ambivalence with regard to the point. The overall context which he has presented would suggest little way to evaluate an act as absolute evil, directed positively against the good. This is particularly true because the basis of his formulation of the problem of morality has so strongly depended upon the preservation of the interests of the individual agent. We find here another respect in which his affiliation is with Aristotle rather than Kant. (Aristotle's grounding of ethics in the desideratum of happiness was for Kant merely an expression of heterogeneous will.) Occasionally Miller seems simply to embrace this consequence: "It seems to me not obvious that any clear account has ever been given of the possibility of deliberate evil. I do not know the arguments which validate self-destruction."[17]

However the problem for Miller will not rest there. He continues, "Traditionally, evil is located in the deliberate assertion of one's own authority, of the authority of one's wants. It is supposed, then, that evil is lawlessness, the separation of one's desires from the law" (pp. 7–8). This formulation does not satisfy Miller, but the specter of deliberateness in evil continues to haunt him. The problem is how to make room for this possibility in a framework that does not distinguish absolutely between the legislative and conative dimensions, the one a level at which the law is generated and the other a level of fugitive desire in need of extrinsic domination. In such a conception, why would creatures of desire want to conform to law? Miller, again speaking for the tradition, finds its ambiguous response: "Desire is said to be fulfilled in the law" (p. 8). Here is Miller's conclusion: "For this answer to be tolerable the law must, however, originate in desire itself. In that case desire is not, in principle, hostile to the law" (p. 8).

Where does this leave us? A positivity of evil cannot be generated from an absolute opposition between rationality (or its product, the law) and desire. Miller still must hold central the conviction that it is the efficacy and integrity of the act which is decisive. And the act, no mere formality, comes into play only within the life of desire. If the impact of rationality can be felt here, then, it must be as part of an effort to secure "an order of all one's desires" (p. 8). Moreover, such an effort can hardly be dictated from above or performed in the abstract. It is a living problem, full of stops and starts, profoundly experimental. In a context of this sort, some error is inevitable. It is in this respect that Miller finds a decisive positive constitutional basis for evil: "Sin is necessary in the free life. It is the mode of acceptance of limit" (p. 12). Now the import of this admission must be thought through by integrating it with the overall context of living desire, to witness how this desire allows for deliberate elements that are not integrated with its primary purposive flow.

"Nobody knows what the emergencies of life will put before him. Sin occurs when one meets an emergency, a personal demand which violates the meaning of that demand itself . . . One may deliberately do it as evil . . . And one does not wholly disavow the practices . . . since, like virtuous acts, they have their validity in the present, in the need of having now something that one wants, or something that allows one to work, to stimulate the imagination" (p. 9).

So the source of positivity in evil is nothing other than the positive role it plays in the conative striving of a personality constantly testing its own limits, its potential for action, its innermost need to be. Personality is a continuous interweaving of dispersed and fragmentary filaments; the synthesis it represents takes the good with the bad. This gives a proto-psychological account of the origin of evil without making evil itself, except as an inevitable result of limit and finitude, an ontological principle. In this respect, Miller rejoins the Western tradition, which finds in evil ontologically speaking not a position but a privation of being. The general orientation of humanity is to fullness of act and being. This is what Miller understands as the good. But of course the good is never desired "in itself" any more than evil is; since there can be no direct commitment to either abstraction, their opposition is not primordial. It is only in the context of an actual commitment to some recognized version of the good that evil, as a particular aberration, can arise: "Evil can occur as sin, as deliberate, only to the person who possesses virtue as part of his life and desires" (p. 10).

The problematic of evil, then, is finally resolved by means of an appeal to the fundamental character of human striving: centered in the immediate interests of a self never fully constituted and always reaching out to the factors that appear to aid in its self-constitution, striving is always vulnerable even to error that in the most intimate and decisive sense attributes fault. Ontologically speaking, the self itself is a fault, an ontological lacuna or gap in the plenum; for it, the fullness of its own being is a task. Within this task, its responsibility extends to everything done or left undone. Even ignorance, when it finds a context to exhibit itself, is revealed as a moral failing. The self, for Miller, carries the grave burden of its finitude in all of its many dimensions. But the journey is not entirely a solitary one. For Miller recognizes very well that the compact analysis of the ontological constitution of individual self-making exhausts neither the whole spectrum of intelligibility of human action nor the moral situation itself. What broadens this horizon in the cultural sphere is the factor of history. What broadens the horizon in the moral sphere, and in fact gives to this sphere its most distinctive character, is the question of the other person. It is to the convergence of these areas, then, that one is led in further pursuing the problematic of Miller's ethics.

Notes

1. Johann Gottlieb Fichte, *Science of Knowledge (Wissenschaftslehre), with the First and Second Introductions,* trans. Peter Heath and John Lachs (New York: Appleton-Century-Crofts, 1970), p. 12.

2. Johann Gottlieb Fichte, *The Vocation of Man,* trans. Rodrick Chisholm (Indianapolis, Ind.: Bobbs-Merrill, 1956), p. 96.

3. Fichte, *Science of Knowledge,* p. 12.

4. Immanuel Kant, *Critique of Practical Reason,* trans. Lewis White Beck (Indianapolis, Ind.: Bobbs-Merrill, 1956), p. 28.

5. Immanuel Kant, *Groundwork of the Metaphysic of Morals,* trans. H. J. Paton (New York: Harper, 1964), p. 62.

6. Kant, *Critique of Practical Reason,* pp. 52ff.

7. Immanuel Kant, *Religion within the Limits of Reason Alone,* trans. Theodore Greene and Hoyt Hudson (New York: Harper, 1960), pp. 15–39.

8. The most developed form of Schopenhauer's view is in Arthur Schopenhauer, *The World as Will and Representation,* trans. E. F. J. Payne, 2 vols. (Indian Hills, Colo.: Falcon's Wing Press, 1958), 1:271ff. An interesting early commentary on Kant's position is found in Schopenhauer, *On the Basis of Morality,* trans. E. F. J. Payne (Indianapolis, Ind.: Bobbs-Merrill, 1965), p. 99. Nietzsche's even darker view of will and power can be discovered, among many other places, in Friedrich Nietzsche, *Beyond Good and Evil,* trans. Walter A. Kaufmann (New York: Vintage Books, 1966), p. 36.

9. Friedrich Schelling, *Of Human Freedom,* trans. James Gutmann (Chicago: Open Court, 1936), pp. 26ff.

10. J. W. Miller, unpublished fragment of 4 March 1949, p. 1.

11. Ibid.

12. J. W. Miller, "On Choosing Right and Wrong," unpublished essay of 1976, p. 5.

13. Ibid.

14. Ibid., p. 8.

15. Aristotle, *Nicomachean Ethics,* trans. Martin Ostwald (Indianapolis, Ind.: Bobbs-Merrill, 1962), 3.1.1109b–30ff., pp. 52ff.

16. J. W. Miller, *The Philosophy of History with Reflections and Aphorisms* (New York: Norton, 1981), p. 33.

17. J. W. Miller, "How Is Sin Possible?", unpublished essay of 1949, p. 6. All further quotations from Miller are to this essay and page numbers will be cited parenthetically in the text.

Making the Moral World

Gary Stahl

University of Colorado

THERE are three main difficulties in expounding J. W. Miller's theory of value: first, he did not write one; second, almost everything he says has implications for value; third, his language is by turns elegantly and darkly Heracleitean, then gently conversational, but never ordinary twentieth-century philosophic prose, most of which sounds as if it were translated (badly) from the German.

I begin with a sketch of how his metaphysical and epistemic stances entail a radical theory of value within which "finitude" is the central category. My aim is not to risk hubris by writing the ethics Miller would have/should have written, but to show how his central themes—explicated in detail in some of the other essays of this volume—jointly launch insightful and fecund initiatives for thinking about value. In the course of explicating key concepts, I give paraphrases of some of his most striking language, not in the belief that his meaning can be said again in terms that "mean the same," but simply to ease the transition into his boldly original way of speaking and to suggest partial overlaps or contrasts with more familiar positions.

It is in *The Definition of the Thing* that Miller makes his most systematic description of philosophy as "the science which has no hypotheses,"[1] but is "the study of definition by the process of definition . . . [and hence] . . . the study of the universal fact" (*DT*, p. 41). Thus he quotes with approval Aristotle's contrast between metaphysics and the special sciences which "mark off some particular being—some genus, and inquire into this, but not into being simply nor *qua* being" (*DT*, p. 34). It is from this notion of metaphysics as totally inclusive that he chides Locke for "assum[ing] special facts, thereby invalidating . . . [his] conclusions" (*DT*, p. 18). Thus "Locke, by making mind and object separately definable and interacting entities, put them into the hands of the scientist, for the laws in accordance with which such special entities interact are discoverable only in the usual way" (*DT*, p. 19).

If one begins, as Locke and so many others do, with any of the usual suspects—with mind and body or organism and environ-

111

ment or subject and object, then the fate of Humpty Dumpty awaits, for "once the split between inner agent and outer fact is made not all the king's horses and all the king's men can patch together the pieces" (*DT*, p. 72). The fundamental ontological category must be process, not those elements which come to be distinguished in process. Although he criticizes Dewey on this very point of assuming a factual dichotomy of subject and object ("What reason there is for basing philosophy on organic response rather than on sunset colors he [Dewey] does not declare," *DT*, p. 21), nevertheless, one of the clearest parallels to Miller's position is Dewey's notion of *transaction*, for there self and other "do not name items or characteristics of organisms alone, nor do they name items or characteristics of environments alone; in every case they name the *activity* that occurs of *both together*."[2]

Accordingly, for Miller, neither persons nor the worlds within which they act are intelligible apart from the processes within which they mutually define and codetermine one another; we do not first find self and world as independently given entities, then face the problem of bringing them into some nonarbitrary relationship. Failure to see this point leaves us suspended between two alternatives, each hostile to an adequate morality: either men are faced with the demand that—for some odd motive—they should conform themselves to rules simply "found" in the world, and thus surrender their freedom. Or, in the opposite scenario, men find themselves free agents in a world which is indeed without rules but which is also an indifferent world which gives neither guide nor sustenance to their deepest commitment and hopes. Miller argues that from the perspective of an adequate metaphysic, both questions dissolve. As he puts it on the final page of *The Definition of the Thing*:

> The result of the analysis of the thing paves the way to a theory of value though no word of value has been introduced. It makes man at home in the world, makes it his world. Evolution has its inspiration because it shows the potentialities of slime, and because it makes man of the stuff of nature so that brother fire and sister water are not strange denominations. But if man's mind is alien, then we live externally in a cold environment which is alien to our fundamental value. [P. 155]

To speak of man as being "at home in the world" (the Hegelian echoes are certainly deliberate) which is "his" world, is more than a metaphor, for both the world and the selves in it are generated through the same finite and constitutional acts. This means that finitude is a category, that is, "a factor in the verb 'to be.' "[3] As Miller says with his usual felicity, "we play moral finger exercises with hedonism or obligation, but make no music so long as action is itself disqualified" (*PC*, p. 93). But to qualify action as constitutional plunges all agents and the structure of all worlds into the flux of time. Either move faces harsh consequences: if time and the act have no status, the individual is condemned to be an inconstant shadow without consequence (Plato's problem); here the law he obeys is not his own, but an alien other that constrains him from without. How can such a law be both compelling and our own? How can we be, as Saint Paul asks, both "under the law and yet free?" The alternative way is equally dark, for it seems that if the law *is* our own and freely chosen, we choose at whim, that "Whirl becomes king" in the subjective tumult of conflicting desires and inconstant passions (the problem which, with such constant conjunction, seems to plague the empiricists).

Miller's solution is quite Kantian, a version of what Kant might have said if he had studied with Darwin, rejected the mechanical analysis of nature, put (like Cassirer) the categories in history, and thought of the moral self not as out of time—banished to the noumenal realm in which act is impossible—but as in a distinctive kind of moral time which only history and act can generate.[4] In essence, Miller works out a process account of how we can be "both subjects and legislators in the Kingdom of Ends." The core is the act which articulates finitude, for "in the living moment of assertion resides the true absolute. It describes no *fait accompli,* but an endeavor, and a procedure. When that will knows itself it becomes social, for its freedom can escape subjectivity only as it recognizes its limitation in the will of others" (*PC*, p. 41).

There is "no *fait accompli,* but an endeavor" because both as acting through the "living moment of assertion" and as acting through the actual and institutionalized "will of others," man is unfinished and vulnerable, "a risky, but creative adventure" (*PC*, p. 105).[5] Here Miller quotes, as he did so often in his college lectures, Ortega's summary judgment that "Man has no nature; he has only a history" (*PC*, p. 105).[6] Within the Western tradition, this is the odd view out, for, as Miller notes regretfully, he did not "find a constitutional incompleteness put forward in any of the types of philosophy. The only discourse that expresses it is history, where there is something less than a *fait accompli* and something more than atomistic unorder."[7] As we shall see, the "something more than atomistic unorder" is found in those local institutions which, as embodied act, give the conditions of controlled and responsible action. So conceived as shot through and through with time, the person has no "environment," no ahistoric locus within which he occurs as a datum: "Let what is considered an act appear as an environed event, and it will disappear into the circumstance in which it is allegedly found. There, its autonomy will be nullified" (M, p. 17). This parallels Kant's insight that there is no room in the Newtonian world of mechanistic causes for the autonomous self; but since for Kant this world exhausted the temporal, no alternative was left for him but to banish the moral self from time, thus making impossible any account of the moral processes though which growth and creativity were possible. Miller's move is quite the opposite: he so embraces finitude that act, far from being absorbed and nullified in nature as alien, is its very source: "For nature . . . is no datum. It is, perhaps, environment, but even as environment the extension of will. Nature, as order, is pure act. Physics is a study of the general conditions of action" (PC, p. 83).

Where action is generative of the actual and finitude is a category, the personal pronoun is not a denotative word that points to a simple and atomistic lump, but what Miller calls an "organizational word" (M, p. 8). Hence moral theory cannot begin with a person—the denotatum of some noun or pronoun—who exists and is knowable, but who then must be brought into relationship with other persons or with some moral order. For in that case any emerging relationship would be posterior and accidental. In a world described on these assumptions, any choice would lack authority; any motive would be either (as Bradley pointed out) reductive—choosing the moral for some nonmoral reason—or circular. Consequently, to be a person is not to be the denotatum of a noun, but a present participle making self and world actual in time.

Let us put this matter, as both Kant and Miller do, in terms of nature: "The order of nature is not an adjective, a property of a *prior* object. Nature and its order are inseparable. Nature *appeared* as order. No one said. '*There* is nature, and upon examination, we find it quite orderly'."[8] In a quite similar way, and for quite the same reasons, persons and the moral order are "inseparable": persons and a moral order appear and are identified only in a formal order generated through act. The question, Why ought I be moral?, disappears if moral action is a condition of my being a self who can freely choose. (What does not disappear is the question of how I can be both free and evil. See Stephen Tyman's discussion in this volume.)

The formal order within which persons come to be is that of the midworld where the "functioning object is that immediacy which embodies the verb—organism, yardstick, clock, balance, number, word" (*PC,* p. 128). These functioning objects of the midworld generate the formal order of nature through acts such as counting and measuring "that are the actual vehicles of order and are so affirmed" (*DP,* p. 141). Any act making such an affirmation "becomes constitutional. It projects a *world.* Any world, any order, is the *form* of the pure act" (*DP,* p. 142). The history of philosophy has quite generally and consistently failed to recognize this ontological process: "The great distinctions have had no presentation. Such has been the lack of the great 'categories' from the earliest time to Kant. We have had Space, but no yardstick; Time, but no clock" (*DP,* p. 59).

Accordingly, the question for ethics is this: what is the moral equivalent of clocks and yardsticks, of counting and measuring? Miller's answer is clear in outline, but not worked out in detail. Basically, he argues that acts toward others (or self) disclose the mutually systematic limits of what it means to be a person in relation to another person (or oneself); these limits, i.e., the conditions of control, are embodied in institutions which are the "residue" of action and its embodiment in the midworld.

Take an example: in the institution of promising I bind my present self—out of respect for both the other and myself—to a specific future. This act affirms both who I am and the shape of the moral time and space through which I act. By defining myself in terms of what I am not yet (myself as fulfilling the promise), I set moral limits to what I can do without contradicting who I am (so far). Since all acts are in principle repeatable (any material maxim can be generalized), any act of promising is potentially an institution: "In all institutions there is a claim to control, to knowledge of truth and of values . . . They bind the endeavors made in time and finitude to eternal truths and values."[9] (This odd phrase, "eternal truths and values," can only refer to the absolute status of the agent's commitment, *not* to some ahistoric status of truth or value. See below, p. 118; also, James Diefenbeck's essay in this volume, pp. 53ff.) Here the institution of promise-keeping is a functional object in the midworld. And where its "binding" is moral and sustains freedom, it is the *condition* of individuality and immediacy, not their negation: "It is law that makes an immediacy possible. Law does not externally regulate the identifiable datum; it is rather a condition of its discovery. The historic distinction of Kant's ethical proposals rests on his assimilation of personal identity with the social bond" (*PH,* p. 180).

Kant's (and Miller's) "assimilation of personal identity with the

social bond" is the key to answering both the problem of motivation and that of freedom. Limiting one's actions by a respect for
others does not destroy freedom, for it is only through such
control that individuality itself is possible: "The will is the force
that commits us to the modes of systematic order. That is the
reason the will is free. It does not give us what we want, but holds
us to those endeavors which permit the emergence of law (*PC*, p.
188). What is shaped by law is the motion of ongoing life, not
some mysterious moral motive which is a One apart from the
Many motives rooted in our inescapable activities, for "a will
cannot . . . find its own clarity apart from the circumstances in the
face of which it is maintained" (*PH*, p. 28).

Our problem is to see how agency, and ultimately moral agency,
is rooted in and emergent from biological and psychological process. What must be avoided is the "widely accepted psychological
reduction . . . [in which this] . . . alleged agency is to be 'explained'
by showing that no agency existed, not really" (*DP*, p. 39). One
mode of reduction is to dissolve everything psychological or dis-
tinctly human into the bit parts of physics; another is to reduce
mentality to some list of instincts as "atomistic urges" (*DP*, p. 40).
But even at this level, Miller argues (in a brilliant chapter that
exemplifies the power of his analysis) for the priority of process.
"Instinct," he insists, "refers not to the substance of an urge, but to
its status" (*DP*, p. 41). Any such status will be an equilibrium
among the revisions and conflicts of activity. Thus "instinct, spontaneous activity, is the locus of learning. It opens up the environment of the organism. Learning and environment are correlative
terms, that is, mutually implicative. Learning does not assume
environment, but generates it" (*DP*, p. 45).

This process of generation is grounded in a "basic and uncon-
scious vitality" (*DP*, p. 119) which gives the organism a "momentum" (*M*, p. 14) within which historical and moral action
occur as a "revision" (*DP*, pp. 32ff.) of ongoing process. Here
historical action is the verb to which the moral is an adverbial
qualification, for morality occurs only *within* history: "history is
not moral: it sets the stage for particular moral systems" (*PH*, p.
145; see below, p. 119, for the difference between morality as a
relatively static moment in process, and as moving and unfinished
process). But organisms *are* agents only as they are *within* history:
there is no hypothetical point at which they stand apart from
history and decide whether to seek and risk within it. "Action
proceeds from limit, and it arrives at no finality, but only at
another defective result. Yet defect, in principle, has no critic.

There is no platform beyond limit from which one may snipe at it"
(*PC*, pp. 88–89). Hence criticism is intelligible only from the point
of view of those formal conditions which are necessary for the
ongoing revision of action.

Vitality and momentum provide the contingent ends which, in
their systematic revision, are a condition of action in history.
Revision is essential, for succeeding or failing in regard to some
fixed and finite purpose is not yet to enter history: "History deals
with acts. Hence, with purpose. But it deals with purpose as the
process that revises it, not as the process that executes it" (*DP*, p.
32). Particular purposes could always be otherwise, and hence
cannot be the source of any such compelling and inescapable
modes as history or morality. Thus neither can be defined in
terms of a set of concrete ends or goals, whether rooted in some
static nature or some ahistoric rule: "history avoids finality, establishes finitude, defines the relatively static, emerges from commitment, allies us with evil, and presents the universal as self-revision
in terms of the necessary" (*PC*, p. 92). In the absence of an
ahistoric context within which history occurs, and which furnishes
ends in terms of which it can be judged, there is no alternative
(chaos aside) but that judgment must be *within* action and in terms
of the formal structures which support action and its critical
revisions.

This same *formal* characterization in terms of the sustaining
structure of will holds of morality, even though—indeed because—morality must involve some concrete commitment within
time and history: "That morality occurs in limit and only there,
that it is not the reaching for a timeless value but for some
present, incarnate, and imperfect good, may seem a strange doctrine. But in that way a philosophy of history is extended into the
region of ethics" (*PC*, p. 88). The commitment must be to "some
present, incarnate, and imperfect good" because only then is the
local act in its irrevocable finitude given generative and constitutional status. And the description of the commitment must be in
formal terms, since "every specific act emerges from a matrix of
commitment, a commitment necessary in principle, but accidental
in its content" (*PH*, p. 33). To say that the commitment is "accidental" does not mean that it is arbitrary in the sense that any choice
will equally do. On the contrary, since this act that generates self
and world risks the possibility of radical ontological failure, it
brings—as a consequence of this possibility of failure—the opportunity for responsible choice: "There is no morality where
nothing finite possesses absolute status. Clearly such a claim

threatens idolatry, but with no less clarity it is also the condition for discovering idolatry" (*PC*, p. 94).

What possesses "absolute status" for the agent is his commitment to the "relatively static as the locus of values and the basis of action" (*PC*, p. 89). Miller explicates this in analogy with Whitehead's notion of the fallacy of simple location: "No location is absolute, but it is just as true that some location must be taken to be absolute in order to make any measurement of relative velocities" (*PC*, p. 89). Similarly, in politics and in ethics, there is no absolute place to stand apart from acts in time and judge them in advance of action. We begin not from inaction and choices contemplated, but *in* action where "every moral judgment rests on the base of a current concern, on what one now identifies oneself as doing" (*PC*, p. 89).

Kant notoriously had trouble getting the agent off dead center and launched into the moral enterprise, and his made-for-the-job notion of "Achtung" seems to have satisfied as few philosophers as has Descartes' pineal gland. But Kant's noumenal agent, unlike Miller's embodied one, had no momentum or vitality rooted in the hurly burly of evolution. "The Kantian morality appears defective on this point. There is no duty nor any rationality until the non-rational and existent moment gives leverage to the moral law. The question 'What ought I to do?' can get no answer, because it makes no sense, until one is already doing something which has for oneself an uncompromising value" (*PC*, p. 89).

This combination of "uncompromising" commitment with "some partial aspect of the actual" inevitably risks what Tillich calls the demonic, which "has happened to religion, to nationalism, and even to education. History rides on the vehicles of partial truth, but their demonry is the sole condition of discovering their force" (*PC*, p. 90). The demonic aspect is disclosed in the systematic inability of these distorted commitments to sustain the conditions of action itself. But this risk is unavoidable: "Life itself is a hazard . . . [which is] . . . absolute, and to that absolute risk there must be an absolute answer" (*PH*, p. 22). There are difficulties, however, in sorting out the precise relationship between judgment in and of history, and moral judgment itself; part of this rests in the fact that the selections in the Norton volumes are neither dated nor identified as to source (letter? essay? personal reflection?). Such clues would be helpful in sorting out changes in Miller's thought or language which reflect a different time or context or audience. So in some texts I have the sense that Miller is his own audience, musing to himself some early morning with a yellow legal pad and a pen, and not engaged in the kind of external dialogue that requires definitions or transitions, or marks the shifting senses between different uses of the same term.

Thus he will often speak of any action as involving values and freedom simply as action in history, and at other times he will mark off moral action as a subset of action within history. I think there are two senses of morality involved here. First, there is morality as a sort of snapshot of a moment of process, catching the residue of moral action frozen into mores. Here the moral is constituted by institutions and commitments which set the essentially fixed locus for action at some particular time and place: "Morality is a concept of the relatively static. It assumes action within an outlook. It does not apply to the revision of outlooks" (*PH,* p. 143).

In contrast, the second sense involves morality as a process where "revision is the redefinition of the moral, not its detailed execution" (*PH,* p. 145). Detailed execution is the merely technical, the pursuit of ends that could have been otherwise, and is not the locus of either compulsion or freedom. Since this inclusive sense of the moral as process applies to both moral and immoral actions, it tends to dissolve or blur the differences between morality and history.[10]

Clearly the moral careers of individuals and groups will involve both phases of relative consolidation and phases of fundamental challenge and change. But the second sense is fundamental, for the relatively static *is* and must be judged *as* an extended moment, an equipose of forces within ongoing processes; but process itself is not the illustration in time of what is static and timeless. As Miller puts it, in one of his favorite phrases, "one does not stand on an Archimedean platform and snipe at the universe or absolve oneself from time in order to estimate the value of its disclosures" (*PH,* p. 83).

It must be the static sense of morality that Miller has in mind when he says that "there is no moral judgment upon history" (*PH,* p. 145), for this would neatly illustrate his argument that "historical events are not to be judged by ahistoric criteria" (*PH,* p. 83). From *within* history, of course, judgment is unavoidable, systemic, and essential. In a fundamental and ontological sense, history *is* the process within which judgment as the self-criticism of free agents can be maintained: "In sum, history is action, and action is will, and will is both purpose and the revision of purpose, and the revision of purpose is freedom, having no end other than the maintenance of action itself" (*PH,* p. 35).

The "punishment" for failing to maintain action "is the loss of the capacity to make history, to come to an end of a self-defining task in which lies all compulsion and all universality. These are the reasons why we cannot escape history" (*PC*, p. 88). It is because of its relationship to universality that this compulsion does not negate agency, but makes it possible: "For the universal is the form of limitation and in all its modes declares the order of critical finitude" (*PC*, p. 88). And critical finitude is the way autonomy emerges in time. Thus, it is only by making an absolutely risky commitment to some finite enterprise that one institutionalizes a world of limits within which self can be articulated. Just as the order of nature emerges out of counting and measuring, so the order of will in its otherness emerges out of the moral acts of which institutions are the embodiment and the condition.

Man is not finished nor his necessarily utopian goals fixed: "As a result, one is thrown back upon some intrinsic validity of the will itself, not for a certification of its value by some result external and accidental to it. We can only assert value, we cannot *attain* it or *prove* it" (*PC*, p. 58).[11] This is to say, in the traditional terms that Kant uses, that the judgment is not *determinant*, which it would be only if "the universal (the rule, principle, or law) is given" and the judgment "subsumes the particular under it."[12] Kant, of course, did see moral judgment as determinant and tried to show how the material maxim must conform to the universal law of reason.

But this way of thinking is incompatible with Miller's claim that ends themselves evolve within the process of will as it is affirmed in the institutions of the midworld. This calls for the form of judgment Kant calls "reflexive," in which "only the particular is given and the universal has to be found for it" (*CJ*, p. 18). The threat, of course, is that without an ahistoric environment of universal ends, will becomes merely capricious, even demonic and idolatrous: "the forces it lets loose seem mad, arbitrary, and uncontrollable" (*PC*, p. 32). This parallels Kant's problem with the judgment of *taste*, which is "not a cognitive judgment, and so not logical, but is aesthetic—which means that it is one whose determining ground cannot be other than subjective" (*CJ*, pp. 41–42). This is *precisely* the problem that Miller embraces—and, I think, meets—in his emphasis on finitude as categorical, where the subject as act is "a factor in the verb 'to be'" (*PC*, p. 142).

Some of the most substantive implications of Miller's position can be seen if we read his analysis of the moral judgment in analogy with Kant's notion of the exemplary judgment. According to such an analysis, we are "suitors for the agreement from everyone else, because we are fortified with a ground common to all" (*CJ*, p. 82). For Kant, that common ground was in the conditions of judgment in general (the fixed categories), but for Miller it must be in the conditions of sustaining free action. Our judgment and our commitment is that some "present, incarnate, and imperfect good" will be *exemplary* of the ways in which human action can be organized and institutionalized to sustain the emergence of agency. Such a judgment, as Kant says, "does not *postulate* the agreement of everyone . . . it only *imputes* this agreement to everyone, as an instance of the rule in respect of which it looks for confirmation, not from concepts, but from the concurrence of others" (*CJ*, p. 23). For Miller, this concurrence of others is the judgment of history, within history: "all history displays this equation between selfhood and actuality. This is the stage on which all action occurs . . . If we can find the actuality which is for us self-defining, and hence absolute, we shall know what to do. Otherwise we may well suffer disintegration and defeat" (*PC*, p. 87).

My guess is that we *will* suffer "disintegration and defeat," either choking on our own filth or incinerating each other in the name of some ahistoric demonology. But if we do make it, then the kind of compassionate intelligence exemplified in Miller's writing and living will be one of the necessities. With it we may achieve some sense of human limits and possibilities which allows us to create a midworld that will sustain us in mutual respect. And if we don't make it, then he will have been an exemplar of what ought to have been.

Notes

1. J. W. Miller, *The Definition of the Thing* (New York: Norton, 1980), p. 17. Hereafter, *DT*, with page references cited in the text.

2. John Dewey and Arthur Bentley, *Knowing and the Known* (Boston: Beacon Press, 1949), p. 71.

3. J. W. Miller, *The Paradox of Cause and Other Essays* (New York: Norton, 1978), p. 144. Hereafter, *PC*, with page references cited in the text.

4. For an attempt to se how much of Kant can be reinterpreted in these process terms, see Gary Stahl, "Locating the Noumenal Self," *Kant-Studien* 72 (1981):31–40.

5. For a brilliant and parallel development of this theme in Heideggerian terms, see Albert Hofstader, *Truth in Art* (New York: Columbia University Press, 1961).

6. The Ortega quote is from José Ortega y Gasset, *History as a System and Other Essays toward a Philosophy of History* (New York: Norton, 1961), p. 217.

7. J. W. Miller, *The Midworld of Symbols and Functioning Objects* (New York: Norton, 1982), p. 125. Hereafter, *M*, with page references cited in the text.

8. J. W. Miller, *In Defense of the Psychological* (New York: Norton, 1983), p. 90. Hereafter, *DP*, with page references cited in the text.

9. J. W. Miller, *The Philosophy of History with Reflections and Aphorisms* (New York: Norton, 1981), p. 181. Hereafter, *PH*, with page references cited in the text.

10. Compare the discussion of status and process theories of the state in *Paradox of Cause*, pp. 37ff.

11. See also James A. Diefenbeck's essay in this volume, p. 47.

12. Immanuel Kant, *Critique of Judgment*, trans. James C. Meredith (Oxford: Clarendon Press, 1952), p. 18. Hereafter, *CJ*, with page references cited in the text. For an analysis of moral judgment as exemplary, see Gary Stahl, "Completing the Past," in *Nuclear Weapons and the Future of Humanity*, ed. Avner Cohen and Steven Lee (Totowa, N.J.: Rowan & Allenhead, 1986), pp. 105–15. When I wrote this, I had not yet read any Miller; had I done so, my article would be richer. I simply have no idea how much of my thinking on this is derived from classes with Miller thirty-some years ago.

III
Relating the Philosophy to Other Disciplines

Miller on Economics

George P. Brockway

I

TOWARD the end of his life, Professor John William Miller several times remarked that he had failed to be convincing in his story of the midworld in terms of physics (yardsticks, clocks, voltmeters . . .), and that he thought it might be more convincingly told in terms of economics (money, exchange, profit . . .). "Money talks," he said. We need not take this judgment seriously, except to the extent that it indicates his concern with economics and with business.

Biographically, this concern goes back to his youth, when, during school vacations, he learned the rudiments of inventory control and cost accounting in his father's lumberyard in Rochester, New York. It continued through graduate school at Harvard, where industrial democracy was an abstractly discussed subject. It both broadened and deepened as he developed his "Philosophy of the State" course at Williams, and culminated during his retirement, when he took pride in managing his own investments. He had not, however, made a thorough study of economics, or of business, and he used to say he wished he had done so.

To be sure, he had not made a thorough study of physics, either. But we may note as an aside that while physicists can be trusted to report intelligently on their discipline, the accounts of economists are likely to be confused, especially as to what they are doing and why. The confusion, which encourages esoteric doctrines, no doubt contributes to the awe with which the public commonly regards the discipline. ("There is more coughing in church," Miller once remarked.)[1] All physicists understand, at least in a general way, what they are doing when they use a yardstick; but a major part of the economics profession considers money an illusion or a veil or, at most, in David Hume's words, "the oil, which renders the motion of the wheels more smooth and easy."

Yet, take away money, and economics collapses. Without money, prices are unutterable. Without money, demand is reduced to psychology and physiology, and supply is reduced to agriculture,

125

engineering, and transportation. Without money, there is no employment except as share cropping or slavery. Money is what Miller called a functioning object. It defines the discipline. Physics is what you do when you measure with yardsticks, clocks, voltmeters. Economics is what you do when you exchange or contract for coin or credit.

If money is a functioning object, then general equilibrium analysis and monetarism, which either treat money as just another commodity or depend on a quantity theory of money, and which together rule the schools and public affairs today, are confused at their core. "Any functioning object is a *declaration*," he wrote. " 'I dub thee yardstick.' So with money. Money has no 'value,' any more than a yardstick has 'length.' "[2]

All standard forms of economics are overturned by this idea; but Miller was too little familiar, or perhaps too impatient, with the winds of economic doctrine to recognize the idea's implications for the schools. He could write, "Gold is the economic dropout. Within an economy no object or service has an intrinsic value. It has only exchange value at a place, time, and for personal desire. . . . Gold is an attempt to make the market incidental, to evade it. Gold has no economic discipline. It tries to command but not to obey."[3] Or more specifically: "As is said, 'money does not grow on trees.' No *'object'* under the heavens—or in Heaven—is money."[4] Yet he could, in almost the same breath, praise Milton Friedman because "he seems to claim that one is not to do as one likes with money,"[5] thus overlooking the fact that Friedman's whole message was that money has a quantity whose growth can and should be controlled arbitrarily, and that this was the only control to which the economy should be subject.

On a related topic he wrote, "I have never felt that I knew for certain what controlled one's attitude toward [inflation] . . . . It seems that neither inflation nor deflation nor stability can be clear ends in themselves, but that they are either accidents or else consequences of some other purposes which entail them. I do not say, or see, that *every* purpose which entails inflation is evil, or that every purpose aimed at stability is good. . . . I must admit to a feeling of the absurd when I hear that, to avoid inflation, some men must not have jobs. This seems to me a sober-sided folly and a real grotesque. . . . I can't trace this out, but my suspicion is that *any* condition of the value of coined money is political. I would find it hard to believe that a government could issue money of *any* sort and then, so to say, let 'nature,' in the form of economics, take its course."[6]

In other words, economics is not a natural science, even though it is generally taught today as an analogue of mechanics. Physics would collapse if the validity of its propositions depended on what someone felt about them; in contrast, economics would not arise if no one wanted any proposed good. Using an example of which Miller was fond, there is nothing right or wrong about the solar system. But an economic system is a system of human beings and has ethical consequences and controls.

II

In early 1976, Professor Miller and I exchanged several letters and had several conversations on economics. I visited him in Williamstown on January 23, and the next day wrote him a letter, in the course of which I said, "As a market is an abstraction of exchange, money is an abstraction of barter." I gave examples from anthropological accounts of ancient Greek gift-giving and the Tlingit potlatch.

He reacted strongly in a letter: "Theology, physics, psychology—the Big Three—know nothing about money. . . . Money, like a yardstick, is a unit of account. Account of what? There is no *apriorist* state of affairs to which a yardstick applies. It *announces* the order of which it is the unit of account. Money announces the order of what is called trade. Trade is a doing. So is measuring."[7]

Before I could reply, he wrote me again: "I can make no *philosophical* statement about money—or anything else—if money is to be a variant in a prior state of affairs, an episode in the experience of assumed persons, Greeks and Indians, identifiable as persons whether or not they have any money or engage in 'exchange.' "[8]

In the meantime I sent him an essay by the British banker and economist R. G. Hawtry. This time his response approached vehemence. "[T]here have," he wrote, "been attempts to see the state as a derivative of a condition prior to any commanding sociability. . . . Hawtry asks the reader to suppose 'that a society is civilized and that money does not exist.' Then quite rightly, he concludes that the unit must be something 'wholly conventional and arbitrary' . . . . How [that alleged society] ever got to be civilized is a question not to be raised. . . . The proposal is that now that we are civilized we can arbitrarily invent money, credit, debt, banks. Nothing, of course, requires us to do so, any more than one could be required to play tennis under its peculiar 'conventional' rules. Is it not rather outrageous that as a member of a prior civilized society I should be expected to pay my debts? . . . Do you expect me, at 81, and with angina pectoris, to play tennis? Why not, on Hawtry's premises?"[9]

We do not choose to use money, any more than we choose to pay our debts, which are denominated in money. Our civilization is not at our option. It could not exist without money, not because money is a great convenience, but because our civilization came into being with money, and not otherwise. The society imagined by Hawtry is meaningless, and its institutions are shams.

This is not to say, however, that at any point in history the meaning of money has been fully disclosed—not in seventh-century B.C. Lydia, not by the money changers in the Temple, not by the Medicis and the Fuggers, not by Adam Smith, not by yesterday's action of the Federal Reserve Board. There have been turning points. "The bourgeois was a puzzle to the medieval classification of noble, clergy, and peasant. He did not fit. Consequently he operated as a revolutionary. 'Laissez faire' was a revolutionary revision of the individual."[10]

Thus economics is something new under the sun, and for that reason it is historical. In economics money is a functioning object. As object, it can be almost anything—a lump of electrum stamped in Lydia, a sheaf of tobacco in colonial Virginia, a blip on a computer screen today. In its functioning it defines, not impersonal processes, as does a voltmeter, but persons who buy and sell. Greeks assuredly used money and bought and sold, but with them the activity was *oikonomia*—household management. It concerned their comfort, even their physical existence, but not their personal self-definition. *Oikonomia* described a relationship to nature, not to society or between men. Miller wrote, "Business resembles architecture in that it is also a mode of the midworld, i.e., a disclosure of 'man'—not of an abstract man, but of individuals, at a place, a time, and already active in other self-defining ways. . . . All modes of self-discovery come to notice as conflicts. Is identification as a businessman tolerable if one has been calling oneself an artist, an Athenian, the son of Ariston, a searcher for salvation?"[11]

"[N]either the altars of the gods," he wrote, "nor the three 'estates' of the medieval world proposed 'economic man' as definitive of man. Trade has been disparaged. . . . [F]or most of Western history the economic man has had no status in the structure of society. Nor did he appear in science, or in heaven. Business had no place in the Nature of Things, nor was it an essential factor in the individual or in the community of supposed individuals. . . . I have to say abruptly that the individual has not been viewed as self-defining and self-maintaining. In 'nature' there is no entrepreneur, no buying and selling, no contractual obligation, no credit, no debt, no money, no society. An economy is our own doing, an order, if any, of our own maintaining."[12]

In other words, "Economics arises when relations with nature are abandoned for relations with society."[13] This abandonment is very recent and systematically incomplete. There is more to life than economics.

III

The economic order has yet to be grasped by most economists, who still are concerned with what they call the efficient allocation of scarce resources (which is another way of saying the struggle with nature), and who deem the object of that struggle the satisfaction of wants and wishes. Miller wrote, "No view of economics based on psychology, i.e., on the 'wants' and 'desires' which turn up in Chapter I of all—or most—treatises on economics, can show any color of authority for making a demand on society."[14] In one of his favorite metaphors, the stream of consciousness has no banks.

In contrast, "What is sold in a market is a clue to people."[15] Consequently, "The market is one of the expressions of the ethical life. The market is not moral or immoral. It is an activity through which moral and immoral practice is made possible. None of the foundations of freedom is moral or immoral. No one can do either right or wrong apart from the mode of independent self-maintenance."[16]

Self-maintenance he called "the original honesty. It is the birth-place of finite authority and respect. There is nothing to respect in any man who does not eat the bread which his own energies have made available. In eating the fruits of his own labor he bears indisputable witness to his own will to live, and to live on his own authority, beholden to none. This is the elementary and fundamental locus of all freedom. . . . It is only for the self-maintaining man that the state is a necessity. For all others it is a tool or convenience."[17]

He seems here almost to be preaching the gospel of the self-made man, but he also wrote, "The defenders of privacy do not, as a rule, understand that the state can have authority over all only in so far as it becomes demanded by all as a prolongation of their own personal force. Consequently, the tories, in defending privacy, deprive themselves and others of the reason for accepting and defending the laws through which self-maintenance can be made increasingly universal. For that reason, the political society which they propose can only be viewed as the guardian of the arbitrary."[18] On the other hand, he was "hostile to *all* alleged criticism which poses as external to the action criticized. I am hostile to the superior moralizers, to the 'arm's length' pose of *The New York Times,* to that supercilious monocle of *The New Yorker,* to the moral drop-outs who proclaim their invulnerable 'conscience.'"[19]

Adam Smith's criticism he held to be likewise external: "Nature launches [the economic condition], and the invisible hand guides it to each one's advantage. But this advantage does not define a *common* good. . . . Men are *alike,* as stones are alike in not being water, but their community is no part of the 'nature' which accounts for their economic connections with others. Similarly, no man joins others in the beneficial result produced not by *his* hand, but by an alien and 'invisible hand.' That result is not *our* doing. As economists [i.e., economic agents] we are impotent both in the self-satisfying activity and in its beneficial outcome. I note that there is no common enjoyment: Lazarus gets no enjoyment because Dives feasts."[20] Smith's invisible hand provided psychological satisfactions, which, because they were merely psychological, were merely private.

Miller's steady theme was, "The free market is a social norm because it is a condition of the free society. It is not an abstract condition, but one associated with other functions of the free individual, which it supports and which, in turn, make it necessary. Tampering with the free market is, then, the occasion for defining a non-economic value, but always a social value, not a private value or the values of a mass of subjective conspirators. Any society must depend on its over-all integrity in order to keep a place for the market. But it must also seek to extend the area of personal and economic freedom as the sole evidence of its own universal ideals. Free trade as an abstract purpose does not define economy, but destroys it. . . . I believe that the free market must always be a local market, and that its extension over a whole nation, and among nations, is an ideal, never quite realized, but only progressively attained."[21]

"The market is not an expression of an abstract law of nature. It is rather a corollary of a will, or a resolve, to establish here and now the conditions of personal independence and effectiveness.

This will or resolve takes many forms. But always it is associated with local and political conditions. . . . Trade is not a scientific or biological phenomenon, but a historical act."[22]

"The defense made by capitalists of the free market is absurd and dangerous. They say that it produces more goods, that it satisfies our desires. For some it does, for others it does not. Of course the communists use exactly the same arguments. If the free market is only a technical device, the heat engendered in its defense or attack becomes ridiculous."[23]

IV

The self-maintaining man, or economic agent, was a 'surd'—an expression Miller adopted from Frank Knight, professor of economics at Chicago, with whom he participated in a 1948 symposium at the University of Chicago.[24] Knight probably meant something like Keynes's man with "animal spirits"—someone who happened to enjoy business and engaged in it regardless of prudent aversion to risk or demonic drive for profit. For Miller, the economic agent was a surd, not because of his inexplicable psychology, but because individuality is constitutional—not subject to explanation. Either way, of course, the surd by definition confounds analysis.

It is fair to say that, like Knight and Keynes, Miller was more concerned with the entrepreneur than with other economic agents. Economics was a modest subplot in his "Philosophy of the State" course in the mid-1930s, and entrepreneurs were essentially the only active actors. Entrepreneurs defined their wills by competing with each other in the free market. The market was, to all intents and purposes, passive. Fully the first third of the "State" course was devoted to "How we meet other minds," and nature figured as the arena for that meeting. Although Miller did not explicitly say so, it seemed that analogously the market would be an arena for the meeting of entrepreneurs' wills.

Both as an undergraduate and later, I used to interpose diffident objections to this scheme, which struck me as having two major weaknesses: first, very few people had an opportunity thus to define their wills; and second, the notorious bottom line, which was the market's self-criticism, was both too vague and too corrupt. I used to insist that, although no businessman, "even a philosopher" could be an economic agent, and that, for my part, I was a book publisher and not an undifferentiated money grubber.

He agreed that the self-maintaining man is not merely a money-maker, but a producer of goods and services, and that his calling, whatever it may be, has standards he upholds and redefines. "One may want to publish books, study philosophy, cure diseases, fly a plane, interpret the law. Apropos of such concerns one earns a living. But such concerns are not accidental wishes but ways of functioning. Functioning brings identity as an agent, both to oneself and to others. Without this factor," he added, "the debate with communism is only a row over technique."[25] Or as he put it another time, "The ground for accepting an economic system is not economic."[26]

Yet functioning seemed still the province of managers of firms that produced competitively in the marketplace, leaving their employees, housewives, government servants, the unemployed, and millions of others without status. After forty years he accepted the point (I cannot say he had not accepted it earlier). "It appears," he wrote, "that few would be free if only businessmen were free. But while one need not be a businessman, one would, it seems, have to be an economist, i.e., part of an economic order. That order would include anyone who supplied goods or services and received goods and services in return. Angels, e.g., would not be part of that order. Nor would the newborn infant, the very sick, the mad, the solitary person eating roots and herbs, 'wandering alone, like the rhinoceros.' "[27] We left it at that, though we had some talk about the meaning of the business enterprise and the household as local controls, and he continued to be wary of consumption as merely the satisfaction of psychological or physiological wants.

"As consumers," he wrote, "we are alone and not in common; what you use (for example, eat) I cannot use. . . . In general, a common good cannot be defined in terms of the consumable properties of separate individuals. Such separation makes and leaves all good merely separate. . . . A good can be common only in case personality is metaphysically common; in case we are members one of another."[28] A common good would not be an exchangeable commodity but a right or duty.

V

Although Miller's interest remained almost exclusively in the producer and the market, and although he was increasingly irritated by those who proposed, in one way or another, to manage the economy, he was by no means an advocate of untrammeled laissez faire. The Great Depression seared the soul of all of his generation and the one following. It was impossible for anyone who lived through it to believe, at least during the event, that the market, though central to economics, was absolute and beyond criticism. Monopoly was an obvious corruption. Even more so was the notion that a man who failed in the market failed altogether—or, for that matter, that one who succeeded in the market succeeded altogether. "Society cannot ask that virtue be miserable," he wrote. And again, "A virtue that society penalizes is not even regarded as a virtue."[29]

Consequently, "Society should not be exploited as a substitute for nature. But, if not, it must appear as guardian of the individual. But to do that without destroying the individual, it must stand as his will to do his job, not to save him from doing it. And so, one must transfer the region of risk from 'purpose' to 'will,' where the penalty of economic loss is compensated by personal honor and recognition. . . . A negative test is this: he will act out of 'will' when he refrains from damaging an enterprise for personal ends. . . . In return, he must have basic security. One must be able to afford basing oneself on 'will.' Society must see that one can work. Then the individual can accept his work without fear."[30] In short, "A man must be able to lose everything, including his life; but he cannot be put into that position by economics. . . . A man can't accept an economic order that kills him."[31]

VI

Reading the lines, and between them, one can see that had Miller indeed made a thorough study of economics, the result would have been substantially different from what is generally taught in the universities and written about in the press. "I notice," he once wrote, "that the *Wall Street Journal* shows great respect for various economic 'laws' as if man observed such laws with the naked eye and the native intelligence, the 'laws' being 'facts,' there for anyone to observe. I'm not prone to see much sense in that."[32]

Throughout his papers there are hints and suggestions that we could wish he had developed. For example: "Depressions are interesting as showing the place where the free economic order fails, and where it fails *in economic terms alone*. . . . One could have a poor nation without finding there a 'depression.'" And this: "Economic values are not the same as human values; economic values are only *commodity* values." And this: "There is no loyalty to the future, only to present values."[33] And this: "There is no such thing as 'the' market."[34]

In the hands of John William Miller economics is not an analogue of mechanics, not a subsidiary of psychology, but an aspect of self-maintenance, self-definition, and hence of justice. It is a normative discipline, proposing standards of right action. Since action is systematically partial, limited, and incomplete, the actions economics proposes are historical. Its problems are in time; its solutions are in time; and so are its failures. Its problems and solutions and failures have become, in our time, fundamental factors of the career of free responsibility.

Notes

The numbers in brackets are first the box number and second the folder number in the Miller Archives in the Williams College Library.

1. Letter to GPB, 22 March 1960 [30, 4].
2. Letter to GPB, 30 January 1976 [31, 4].
3. Letter to Eugene Miller [19, 5].
4. Letter to GPB, 30 January 1976 [31, 4].
5. Letter to GPB, 1977 [31, 6].
6. Letter to GPB, 20 March 1966 [30, 4].
7. Letter to GPB, 30 January 1976 [31, 4]. This central insight of Miller's appears in the first chapter of his doctoral dissertation, *The Definition of the Thing* (New York: Norton, 1980) as well as in notes he made more than fifty years later, when he wrote, "Philosophy is the discourse without an '*a priori*.'" (*The Midworld of Symbols and Functioning Objects* [New York: Norton, 1982], p. 7.) "Inasmuch as a given discourse involves presuppositions, postulates, or hypotheses, it is liable to refutation by an attack on them. The very sort of consideration which makes an assumption reasonable provides the ground for its rejection." (*Definition of the Thing*, p. 14.) A "philosophy" based on assumptions or institutions is either inferior science (and rightly scorned as such) or mysticism (and thus a rejection of discourse).
8. Letter to GPB, February 1976 [31, 4].
9. Letter to GPB, March 1976 [31, 4].
10. Letter to GPB, February 1976 [31, 4].
11. Letter to GPB, 26 February 1976 [31, 4].
12. Letter to Eugene Miller, November 1976.
13. Miller's notes made in 1950s [4, 4].
14. Ibid.
15. Letter to GPB, 19 April 1960 [30, 4].
16. "Economics, Politics, and Ethics," p. 12; July 1949 [3, 6].
17. Ibid., pp. 5–6.
18. Ibid., pp. 6–7.
19. Letter to GPB, 26 February 1976 [31, 4].
20. Letter to GPB, 19 September 1976 [30, 4].
21. "Universal Free Trade," 18 February 1949 [3, 2].

22. Ibid.

23. Ibid.

24. Miller's contribution was "Freedom as a Characteristic of Man in a Democratic Society," in *The Paradox of Cause and Other Essays* (New York: Norton, 1978), pp. 97–105.

25. Letter to GPB, 19 April 1960 [30, 4].

26. Miller's notes made in 1950s [4, 4].

27. Letter to GPB, 26 November 1976 [31, 4].

28. Miller's notes, undated [11, 5].

29. Miller's notes made in 1941 [12, 1].

30. Ibid. By "purpose" Miller here means a specific objective, for example, to manage a factory, to be a teacher, or to drive a truck. By "will" he means revision of the purpose as it proves (as it systematically must) inadequate or impossible. See *The Philosophy of History with Reflections and Aphorisms* (New York: Norton, 1981), pp. 32–36. Will is self-maintenance.

31. Miller's notes made in 1941 [12, 1].

32. Ibid.

33. Miller's notes, undated [11, 5].

34. "Economics, Politics, and Ethics," p. 12 [3, 6].

Literature, History, and What Men Learn

Robert H. Elias

Cornell University

TIME and space have long been accepted as categories that we cannot escape; they underlie every statement we make. We can talk about timelessness but cannot assert it without invoking the very conception of time that we would transcend. We can discuss spacelessness but cannot avoid affirming what we would go beyond. Indeed, we cannot even define "beyond" without asserting the ultimacy of both time and space. It is the same with history. If John William Miller had taught nothing else, he would have exerted a profound influence through his exhibiting history as a category, a dimension of experience without which experience cannot be articulated—even known—meaningfully. The experience of human beings—experience that in order to be "experience" rather than neural responses to stimuli requires the objectification of will—is the context, the matrix, from which perceptions and assertions of all sorts flow.

Some of us who were Miller's students have in print acknowledged the extent, and revealed the range, of the influence he has exerted. I give just a few examples. Walter Kaufmann's *Philosophic Classics, Volume 1: From Thales to Ockham* is dedicated to him. Cushing Strout's *The Progressive Revolt in American History: Carl Becker and Charles Beard* acknowledges his "immensely provocative teaching" in the philosophy of history and quotes a telling statement of his to conclude *The Veracious Imagination: Essays on American History, Literature, and Biography*. George P. Brockway's *Economics: What Went Wrong and Why and Some Things to Do about It* is dedicated to his memory and states that his teaching has affected not only the ideas but also the sentence rhythms and turns of phrase. And two of my own books—*Theodore Dreiser: Apostle of Nature* and *"Entangling Alliances with None": An Essay on the Individual in the American Twenties*—credit him with whatever merit their interpretations enjoy.[1] We obviously have not all shared the same interests, but we have all responded to the same ideas in similar ways and simply singled out for ourselves those that have most immediately met our individual concerns.

For me Miller's ideas shaped, and continue to shape, the study of literature and of the way literature contributes to the rendering of interdisciplinary history, American studies in particular. I had when I entered college assumed that the study of history was a search for causes and that the history of literature was simply a recounting of the way writers were either of, behind, or ahead of their "times." But then in 1935 Miller's arresting essay on "The Paradox of Cause" opened my eyes to the sterility of the infinitely regressive search: I could see the meaninglessness for interpretive projects of the attempt to reach back for the universal cause— "what explains everything explains nothing in particular"[2]—and understand the meaningfulness that would inhere in rejecting cause for purpose as a subject of investigation.

Purpose! It is in his chapter on purpose in *The Philosophy of History* that the ideas that had the greatest impact on me are most lucidly concentrated, published in this volume long after I first encountered them. "History deals with acts," Miller states. "Hence, with purpose. But it deals with purpose as the process that revises it, not as the process that executes it." Acts, he explains, are what one does "in the interests of a more inclusive program." Such a program is already in place, at hand, in progress; one may accept it, reject it, or try to revise it. "The essence of a purposive act is not only that it proceeds from a general program but also that it requires the revision of the program in the interests of which it is undertaken." This means that events, individuals, moments in time "play a role in history only as they involve a revision of the premises of action." What is historical is what affects values, what changes the meaning of the "facts," and leads to new types of action. Action is, then, what history is—it is will, "and will is both purpose and the revision of purpose, and the revision of purpose is freedom, having no end other than the maintenance of action itself." The historian in consequence tells his story "only in terms of what men learn . . . [and] what they learn is history only as they learn about *the conditions of action*—that is, of freedom."[3]

The career of the United States provides an especially happy opportunity for exhibiting the nature of the historical enterprise and its inescapably interdisciplinary substance. Because we are a democratic society, the political forms of whose state are free of tyranny, we can assume a close—indeed, an indestructible—relationship between institutions and individuality, between the ex-pression of the social will and the expression of the individual spirit, so that laws and belles lettres are expressions always of common assumptions, purposes, values, even when writers or painters may be criticizing society. The history of our laws is a narrative of the social will, of the individual in his social relations. The history of our literature is an account of the exploration of the individual in his relations to himself (or to his circumstances) even in those works in which social problems supply the substance of the plot. Our complete history must recount a shared story. When, for example, we talk about the eighteenth century, we should refer, as John William Ward has reminded us, to the American Constitution's celebrated checks and balances, to the balance and symmetry of the architectural forms displayed in our nation's capital, to the ideal of Reason, to the satisfactions of the heroic couplet.[4] Balance, judiciousness, equipoise—connections: literature and politics all of a piece.

Literature may, of course, record and reflect current events, but its contribution to social documentation is only incidental to our focus. Social and political facts primarily create contexts. We don't, to be sure, reject what James Fenimore Cooper's *The Prairie* tells us about pioneer life, or what Nathaniel Hawthorne's *The Scarlet Letter* reveals about the Puritans, or what Stephen Crane's *The Red Badge of Courage* discloses about warfare; but for facts as such we would do better to consult the best journalists, often the more popular writers, who have only facts to report. The cultural com-mon denominator is deeper than social facts; it is embedded in point of view, values, judgments. Cooper, Hawthorne, and Crane in writing of the past tell of their own time as much as they do of their characters' time, for after all, whatever they tell of their characters' time is ultimately colored through their own prisms. Questions of their accuracy are relevant simply as ways of clarify-ing their point of view. Their content does not depend for its significance on timeliness or timelessness.

What is to be focused on, then, is not the topic or subject as a separable item, but the topic or subject as it is defined by its presentation. The endings of Edgar Allan Poe's stories, the cata-logues in Walt Whitman's incantations, the resolution of the plot in Frank Norris's *The Octopus,* the fragmentary structure of T. S. Eliot's *The Waste Land,* the lack of subordinate clauses in Ernest Hemingway's fiction, the first sentences in Toni Morrison's nov-els—these disclose more about cultural assumptions than simple topical relevance does. Facts, of course, do matter, but one can mold them as one chooses. It is always a question of shape. The historian's truth is in the choice of the configuration, whatever the history is to be of.

In its broadest outline the development of the United States suggests what I believe Miller would have regarded as an essentially dialectical process. In the context of our society such apparently opposed terms as liberty and equality, individual independence and national obligation, ethnicity and the melting pot, self-maintenance and social commitment, human nature and human freedom are mutually necessary and repeatedly redefine each other and the ways their tensions should be resolved.[5] We could write, by way of a topic sentence for the total national story, and with the Millerian expounding of purpose in mind: "The white man discovered the North American continent by accident, but he settled it on purpose." The unfolding of this purpose between the fleeting explorations of the early Norsemen and the deep and complex international entanglements of our own day can then be traced in four, perhaps five, stages, leaving us on the threshold of the future's continuation of the process.

To demonstrate the participation of literary expression in this process, I have found it helpful to begin by identifying the stages in terms of our society's changing conceptions of nationhood. In the first stage the colonies become a nation, conscious of themselves as a separate, self-governing entity. In the second stage that entity, that nation, undertakes to define its character as an essentially democratic one, with a good deal of emphasis on egalitarian ideals. In the third stage the society moves toward identifying the maintenance of those ideals with the national interest; and the government, until then nominally neutral, becomes a positive force, an instrument for fulfilling the national interest. In the fourth stage we become self-conscious as a nation among nations: during the Spanish-American war we grope toward this awareness; in World War I we optimistically acquire a role but lack an understanding of its implications and obligations; in World War II we grasp the obligations but lose much of the optimism we enjoyed under Woodrow Wilson; and now—at perhaps the beginning of a fifth stage—we are contending with a need for a radical redefinition of ourselves as a nation among nations.

Stage by stage, we can fill in particulars to confirm that "what [men] learn . . . about *the conditions of action*" has shaped our history. The spirit of independence produces a separate nation dedicated to the values of individualism, whereupon national needs and individual needs come into opposition that is embodied in the disagreements of Thomas Jefferson and Alexander Hamilton. The presidency of Jefferson, by necessity conferring on the president national power, partially resolves the tension and at the same time leads to the supplanting of the aristocratic spirit by an egalitarian one that makes possible the accession of Andrew Jackson, the development of the spoils system, the spread of factions, and with factions, the growth of sectionalism that is doomed to conclude in the Civil War. There has been a good deal of argument about whether that war was a repressible or an irrepressible one. But much of the discussion has been beside the point. The crisis was produced not wholly because of economic differences or disagreements about slavery as a moral concern. It was basically a question of individual commitment: when no loyalty greater than loyalty to a section or region appears, no peaceful resolution of radical conflicts between sections or regions remains possible.

We can continue to fill in, even while recognizing that this particularization is sketchy and schematic. Largely because of Abraham Lincoln the Civil War establishes the necessity of a national government, but it does so through a party that, concerned with the needs of reconstruction, favors finance and industry and believes that these should not be hampered by restrictive laws. At the same time, as the scale of life in the United States becomes enlarged, as individuals increasingly feel themselves citizens of a continental nation as well as of a section or region, the scale of reactions also becomes enlarged. The organization of capital (Caesarism, as Charles Francis Adams, Jr., termed it)[6] and of labor, the nationalizing of political parties, the growth of cities, all produce action on a nationwide scale. The struggle to control the federal government becomes a struggle between those who want it to take positive action against restrictions and those who want positive action for restricting certain activities. Our national government has inescapably assumed a positive, Hamiltonian role for the advancement of Jeffersonian ideas.

The moral fervor attached to this carries into Wilson's statements of our foreign policy, which are unhappily divorced from proper recognition of self-interest. It is not surprising that the postwar decade rejects Wilsonian ideas as hollow, adheres to self-interest without concern for moral and social consequences, and concludes its disengagement with the crash. Franklin D. Roosevelt effectively introduces a reconstituted progressivism, but his legacy seems now to be a commitment to absolute ends rather than to endless process. That is, as we survey our situation today we find a

sort of weariness with many of the complexities of foreign relationships, a failure to discover a place for ideas and self-examina-
tion, a desire to exert power unilaterally—a wish, in short, to
produce solutions rather than to preserve the means for admit-
ting new problems, new clashes, and a future that will indefinitely
produce problems demanding solutions that will forever generate
the consequences of their inadequacies, in turn requiring new
solutions equally insufficient. Yet as a nation we cannot in fact
escape being always in a state of becoming.

What we find in the works of our most highly regarded authors
are concerns and assumptions that they share with individuals
who exert political and financial power. As Arthur M.
Schlesinger, Jr., has noted, the literature of a period tries "to
resolve on the moral and artistic level some of the problems faced
by [the] . . . democracy in politics and economics."[7] He is right.
Our earliest writers, those recording their reactions to the new
world during our first stage, few of them aspiring to qualify as
producers of belles lettres, largely report conditions in order to
satisfy and entice Europeans, to bolster morale, the Southerners
largely describing, the New Englanders interpreting, all perceiving promise. During the Revolutionary and early national period
more seriously literary poets, dramatists, and novelists exhibit a
national self-consciousness that leads them to try to create a literature appropriate to a new nation. We observe this cultural concern among Philadelphians, New Englanders, Knickerbockers.
We think of Philip Freneau, William Cullen Bryant, the Connecticut Wits, Washington Irving, James Fenimore Cooper, Henry
Wadsworth Longfellow. Some of them use historical materials to
communicate patriotic feeling; some attempt to compose epics,
albeit rather abstract ones; some try to define the national promise
and sensibility in ways that lead them to use, often imaginatively,
European forms; yet all are preoccupied with the role of the
individual American in a society hewn out of nature.

Doubtless Emerson's vigorous rejection of the courtly muses of
Europe in "The American Scholar" incorporates the affirmations
that developed during the decades preceding the Civil War. At
the same time, even as Emerson begins to assume the role of
spokesman for a national literature, his premises are subject to the
same sort of criticism as are those of the proponents of Jacksonian
individualism. For the conception of the individual that underlies
Jacksonian politics underlies the plea for transcendental self-re-
liance that rings through much of Emerson's writing. Just as the
Jacksonian Democrats value the nation insofar as it allows individ-

uals to enjoy autonomy—lets them alone, in short—as Herbert Croly persuasively argues in *The Promise of American Life*,[8] so is Emerson an advocate of an individualism that denies and rejects limits. It falls to Hawthorne and Herman Melville to question that outlook. Yet even they, while dwelling as they do on the necessity of fellow feeling, often concern themselves more with sin or evil latent in an individual. Their fiction emphasizes internal resolutions rather than external reconciliations. Only when war ensues do preoccupations with the scope of individualism and the nature of the individual change.

I could at this point discuss the significance of Walt Whitman, whose celebration of the ego embodies Emerson's and whose sense of national identity both limits and transcends that ego in a manner that points to the preoccupation with social life we find in later writing. He builds a bridge to the larger community. (I would want to include Harriet Beecher Stowe in this part of the discussion.) But it is the later writing that I prefer to touch on instead, since it illustrates my argument most succinctly.

After the Civil War our writers shift their attention to conflicts that are centered *within* society, quite different from the transcendental concerns of Emerson and Melville. The sense of nation, of region, of what Robert H. Wiebe has called a distended society[9] is a complex sense. But what is particularly striking in the present context is that we find in Mark Twain, William Dean Howells, Henry James, and many of their contemporaries an interest in writing fiction that undertakes to have their characters come to terms with their country's social conditions, social customs, economic actualities. Such characters define their freedom, what they mean by their selves, what it means to be American, in the substance of their social accommodations: their inner struggles and moral tensions become increasingly a function of social behavior—Howells's Silas Lapham and James's Lambert Strether come to mind as good examples. These writers convey an awareness of their national place; the sense of nationality permeates their scenes and characters' critical decisions. Even the so-called regional or local-color writers dwell on locale or ancestry as distinctive features of the union rather than as features situating them apart from it—Sarah Orne Jewett, Mary E. Wilkins Freeman, Charles W. Chesnutt, for example. They do not necessarily agree with each other. Certainly they are not followers of William McKinley! But, for all the differences in emphasis one may find in their fiction, they do not differ so much among themselves with respect to what they imagine as a social ideal.

It is here that the historian's challenge lurks, here that one is particularly conscious of Miller's discussion of action and purpose. What do these writers and their political leaders have in common? What values do they share, and what ultimate end to their times do they all, in their various ways, contribute to? Their new national feeling has within itself opposition—a spirit of reform energized by the righteous nationalism it criticizes (remember Mark Twain's "To the Person Sitting in Darkness")—and this then becomes the spirit dominating the Progressive Era, which finally generates its own fatality in Woodrow Wilson's moralism.

We could go through each of our historical stages, if we had the space here, to define the conception of self that pervades each period and the thrust toward redefinition that brings the period to a close. I have in my own writing about the American twenties tried to develop such an approach. What do Calvin Coolidge and Ernest Hemingway have in common? What does that have to do with the behavioristic theories of John B. Watson, the public attitudes toward Al Capone and the Sacco-Vanzetti case, the conduct of business, the celebration of Charles A. Lindbergh's flight, the Harlem Renaissance, and the moral reflections of Joseph Wood Krutch and Walter Lippmann? What assertion of individuality, what conception of freedom, what larger purpose can be uncovered in the search for answers? My label is that of the old Jeffersonian prescription of "entangling alliances with none"— radically modified by its shifted context—but someone else's label may be more apt. Whatever the label or generalization, the historian's concern must be to achieve the defining conception, one that will in turn open the way to a definition of what remains historic about the era that follows.

We choose to discuss as historic the ages or periods that are marked by revisions of purpose, revisions of what the inhabitants of the United States mean by freedom, embodied in the relation of the individual to other individuals. Although we may not always find labels that can take account of the innumerable particulars that in their immense variety and range seem to defy the simplifications of verbal summaries, nor simply agree about the boundaries of our periods, we cannot disagree about our criteria. We search to discover the dominating conception and with it the challenge forcing a resolution that will succeed as dominant and provoke its own challenge. Just as in the great novels and dramas, whether tragedies or comedies, the deed comes home to the doer, so in our history our deeds come home, in economic policies, in political commitments, in literary theory and practice, all interrelated. Is it sheer accident that during the past decade the self-reflexivity of a number of serious writers and the deconstructionism of fashionable academic formulators of literary theory share the sporadic solipsistic self-deceptions of a popular president for whom, as Michael P. Rogin has tellingly demonstrated,[10] the world in which actual people really bleed can be replaced by cinematic fictions? Do they not concur in equating the empirical life with everyone's private fiction?

Today we find our literary history in the process of being "reconstructed." Many articles have been written in the last few years on the need to reexamine the canon in order to call into question the attention devoted to white male writers—equally accomplished women, blacks, and other ethnic writers have been unrecognized. The complaints about omissions and assumptions rooted in sexual and racial bias are certainly just, yet the most recent attempt to provide a more comprehensive account of our country's literary accomplishments offers a lot of lumber for the reconstruction but without a frame entirely adequate to bear the weight or supply a design. The introduction to the *Columbia Literary History of the United States* states that the editors

> have made no attempt to tell a "single, unified story" with a "coherent narrative" by making changes in the essays. That is, the editors have not revised the beginnings and endings of essays to create the appearance of one continuous narrative. No longer is it possible, or desirable, to formulate an image of continuity when diversity of literary materials and a wide variety of critical voices are, in fact, the distinctive features of national literature. . . . [T]he history of the literature of the United States is not one story but many different stories.[11]

No one should disagree with this description of what they go on to term "a fundamental tension" between the desire to compose a coherent story and the desire to give play to interpretive diversity. Nor should one stubbornly deny that there are many stories to tell. "Do I contradict myself?" Whitman asks in "Song of Myself" as he merges his bardic voice with the nation's. "Very well then I contradict myself. / I contain multitudes" (ll. 1324–26). Yet there is always that "I"; there is always *the* story of stories. There is always the containment of the multitudes, the diversity underlying which the historian must look for links, even if they should constitute but some agreed-upon definition of the substance of the diversity, variety, and contradictions. The historical narrative cannot be a random compilation of materials that resembles the displays in a secondhand furniture store or flea market. We require arrangers, designers. I suppose that in one sense everyone must be his or her own arranger or designer—or historian. But as historians, literary or whatever, we will not fully meet our obligations if we do not at least draft a blueprint for a model structure, a house in which may be many mansions, even as we recognize that this house will itself eventually become another mansion.

None of this argument ought to be understood as a disparagement of the many richly documented studies and narratives that give us densely textured accounts of our past—the often picturesque renderings of the fabric of American life. Daniel J. Boorstin's marvelously detailed three-volume portrait of the American experience—*The Americans*—is one of the most appealing of recent accomplishments.[12] Written with vigor and wit, Boorstin's volumes are rich in vignettes and information; yet, as I have written elsewhere, they leave us peculiarly deprived.[13] Since his intent is to demonstrate that real history is the record of human adjustments to circumstance, he excludes from attention wars, politics, great decisions, ideas, and values. How did people live? is the question he wants to answer. But his people are essentially passive agents, adjusting to circumstance as ants adjust to barriers heaped in their pathways. We miss an account of what adjustment means, of why his Americans undertook to adjust one way rather than another, of the interests, programs, ideals, or values for which this or that group gave up something in order to survive. We miss that account because Boorstin does not consider it relevant. Survival may be everyone's purpose, all right, and we may always be in the clutch (not always fell) of circumstance; but unlike tropisms, we in fact survive on certain terms that depend on how we view, and re-view, ourselves. In Boorstin's trilogy, then, the Americans have no history as Miller (or I) would define it.

The ideal historian would not reject Boorstin's portrait. The ideal historian would embody its hypnotically compelling details in a powerful conceptualizing synthesis that would constitute the story of stories that the editors of the *Columbia Literary History of the United States* find impossible to tell. Although Miller, when I sent him a copy of my *"Entangling Alliances,"* wrote me that it was "a true history-book,"[14] I do not myself lay claim to being the ideal historian I describe. I have not, on the one hand, provided myself with a Boorstinian treasure chest of details, and, on the other hand, I am no Denton J. Snider, the widely neglected St. Louis Hegelian, whose books about the American state and the Civil War years exhibit a grasp of United States history that Hegel himself would have endorsed.[15] Yet even if I were a Snider, and also had a treasure chest, that would not be enough, as I have just indicated; for we require not only both Snider and Boorstin, but many others from all the academic disciplines as well, who will together contribute the pieces of the jigsaw puzzle that someone with a sufficiently imaginative mind can fit together. Actually, in his more recent *The Discoverers* Boorstin, himself, evinces some of this imaginative spirit. "My hero is Man the Discoverer," Boorstin declares; "I turn . . . [f]inally to . . . the self-discovery of Man the Discoverer":

> This is a story without end. All the world is still an America. The most promising words ever written on the maps of human knowledge are *terra incognita*—unknown territory.[16]

Literary biographers, I would note, confront a challenge similar to the one confronted by literary historians. They must tell the story of how the writer they portray conceives of the individual— the individual's freedom, the good life, if you like—and refines, develops, or revises that conception in work after work. The unfolding is not in terms of explicit propositions, but in terms of artistic elements—tone, plot development, management of time, conceptions of heroism or nobility, voice, theme—all more readily accessible, perhaps, in prose fiction than in poetry but present in all genres nonetheless. Like the historian, the biographer has the immense difficulty of doing justice to the complexities that inhere in being human and at the same time disclosing in the particular complexities of an individual a pattern or meaning. Examples of the difficulty abound: we have the irritatingly reductive biographies and the vast, frustratingly amorphous ones—and the admirable triumphs, perhaps easier for the historian of a single person than for the historian of a whole society or nation.

Insistence on the scrutiny of purpose and its inescapably concomitant objectification in acts launched by definition in a social— rather than, say, cosmic—context implies an approach to literature that stresses what literary historians and biographers must look for when they relate how our writers have progressively clarified the meaning of self and the nature of the society within which the conception of the self becomes actual. Comments in letters Miller wrote me in April 1946 about Theodore Dreiser's *The Bulwark* are illustrative of what he expected in his reading. (I had sent him a copy of the novel, along with the March 1946 issue of *The Book Find News*, which was devoted to the Book Find Club's selection of *The Bulwark* and to which I had contributed a brief article.) I quote at length to avoid the risk of inadequate paraphrase:

[10 April 1946] The result seems to me unclear. In certain religious stories which I read years ago, the prodigal returns to the true faith. Etta, one of the more interesting of the children, weeps at last for "life." This suggests that she is not experiencing the "inner light" which would, I believe, recommend a more hopeful, or, perhaps, more resigned view of "life." The tears may be suitable for Dreiser, but they do not follow from the story. Etta may have become more devoutly Quakerish, or have taken some other turn toward religion, repenting of her "village" days, yet thanking God for His mercy in bringing her at last to the true church. For He works in most mysterious ways.

Etta, then, does not justify her parents. They too seem finally caught in the general folly. But why not "heigh-ho the holly"? But if the parents were not righteous, why the tears and contrition? Etta asks to be "forgiven"; why so? She admits *her own* folly, but should not, then, weep for "life," but for herself.

There seems here no influence of person on person. No individual life rises to the surface. . . . People react to other people because of some subjective interest. . . . Another person should promise something intrinsic, namely the person himself. He should not be a meal-ticket, or a text-book, or a source of adventure, or a guide to new opportunities of whatever nature. This capacity of a person to arrest another person seems to me absent here, and in the "Tragedy" [*An American Tragedy*]. . . .

Dreiser sees persons as part of the universe. . . . Consequently they never appear as persons. There may be a "life force," but it reduces the individual to insignificance, and life itself to the same chaos, so that not even tears are called for. No one gets frustrated. Things are merely what they are. . . .

I used to say that one can't make God an artistic subject. I still think so. Nor can "nature" or "life" or the "life force," or any objectified absolute be so used. Dreiser will not *quite* objectify. He will have pity at last. Years ago I was troubled with that point in Anatole France. I found it poignant, but confused. One has to reassert oneself. At the same time there seems something short of complete objectification in the status of the Quaker faith. Dreiser seems to reach for a reverence which his objectification of the spectacle of life steadily negates.

[23 April 1946] . . . Did I say that God is not a subject for art? Probably so. Nor do I think the Universe can be. Dreiser has quite a bit of concern with the Universe, materialistic or vitalistic.

I agree entirely with your words in the article, that Dreiser, although once a determinist of materialistic sort, exhibited great concern for man. Something had to give way. Man or matter would emerge as dominant. Well, man does, or at least something anthropomorphic. In a novelist that is the likely turn.

There are a number of writers in our time who have taken to religion, after exploring some unstable view of man. Huxley is the example I know best. But religion and philosophy turn on universals. . . .

In art, I feel, man sees himself as an individual. Art does not speak the truth, nor want the truth. Robert Frost so often ends a poem with a moral: "One could do worse than be a swinger of birches"; or, for a change to beginnings, "Something there is that does not love a wall"; or "'Men work together,' I told him from the heart, 'Whether they work together or apart.'" This is like Aesop. It may all be true, but it makes one consider. These are not words of passion, nor feelings expressed and explored because they sweep the personality. There is reservation here, the pondering sage.

The experiences which lead to religious or philosophic truths seem to me not properly aesthetic. Certainly they are intense, moving, generated from commitments, revolutionary, perhaps integrating at last. But they end in a *belief*, and so are subject to the type of examination proper to such beliefs. There are "cosmic" emotions. But they neither proceed from the individual will, nor result in such will. They redefine *all* persons, not specifically the characters in play or novel or poem. They reassess the whole person, not his particular act. . . .

Art seems to me to rest on the embodiment and incarnation of values, not on their ideality. It rests on some *actual* absolute. I think that is why love stories are so successful. Love makes the ideal actual. That actuality can inspire in specific ways. It may transform nature, but the change is from the actual to the ideal, never the other way. There are no religious love stories. . . .

[24 April 1946] Perhaps it comes to this: I do not like novels about the cosmos. I do not think that struggles to clarify one's cosmos are literature. . . .

More positive examples of what literature *is* appear in correspondence occasioned four years later by a discussion he, Edward A. Hoyt, and I were carrying on about William Faulkner. On 19 November 1950, he wrote me:

F's intensity is fascinating. I would like to know more of the ability of his best characters to create—or acknowledge—something like the actual world. Government, business, industry, science, church, nature—all the articulate areas of the common mind—seem obscure or unknown. You mention Conrad; Jim's act [in *Lord Jim*] occurred against the background of institutions with which settlement had to be made, the British merchant service & its traditions, the French navy, the business & private world of Stein, the humanity of Marlowe. The inward had a measure of the outer. In Conrad there is usually a touch, or strong dose of Nature, as in "Typhoon" & "The End of the Tether." In "The Arrow of Gold" the relation of character to institutions and to Nature is at a minimum with the result that the explorations of the hero in the dimension of personal romance become both intense and vagrant. I am always attracted by the intensities, but I do feel that they can be parasitic and diseased when not the source of revelation of an objective order.

As a contrast, I read some of the stories of W. Irving, "Tales of a Traveler." Here there is report, humor, irony. Values already exist and are in control of the world. It is restful to read such a book. Irving valued cultivation. One can see that at a glance. The soul is not always in a desert of loneliness, frustration or desire. Certainly these stories are one-sided. Yet, there is a side to them. An author should show a "world." I feel that Faulkner does not make clear for what world he speaks. . . .

In some way I feel that no man *should* carry the whole world on his shoulders, but should find it there waiting for his acknowledgment. To render that acknowledgment is part of the point of a story. Certainly it is a factor in all humor & irony, in comedy & tragedy. One can not spin it out of one's own consciousness. Something now going on must be admitted & taken into account. That is what I miss in Faulkner. But, as I remarked to Ted [Hoyt], it may be that what F. sees in the South is a lot of people for whom there is just no such authoritative environment. Possibly, it is the intensity of lives whose habits presume an environment quite unknown to them which is the peculiar disclosure of Faulkner. . . .

One can disagree with the interpretation of Dreiser or Faulkner, and one can even find greater satisfaction in reading them than in reading Washington Irving. But if one is to argue in behalf of Dreiser or Faulkner, it will eventually be on Miller's terms: no, *The Bulwark* is not fundamentally about the cosmos; no, Faulkner's characters do not shoulder the whole world but do find a world waiting there for their acknowledgment. Likewise, when Miller is formulating a favorable judgment, one may disagree with the description of what the writer is doing, but have difficulty challenging the premises. A letter to Hoyt on 25 March 1962 provides my last example:

Read again Edith Wharton's "Age of Innocence" and liked it better than ever. Some very good scenes. Her characters have their aches & pains, but the main figures are mature, with a sense of circumstance in which alone can appear both their good & ill. In the love triangle all three take losses, and are well aware of it, and two of them know that the loss is both irreparable and unavoidable. So there is a chance for depth and height.

E. Wharton gets spoken of as a social critic, and no doubt properly. But so is many another. I would say that she is that rarer artist, one who sees the individual. Her sharper people accept both circumstance—the area in which they act—and the consequences of acts in those circumstances. But, of course, this requires the society which is under fire.

Robert Frost, at least in his earlier work, always exhibits character in its environment, or nearly always. Apples have to be picked, hay gotten in, walls mended, vagrants tended. At least such is often the case. In this he is like Wharton.

I don't think it is of prime importance for the artist that these circumstances be always themselves social and secular. They might be cosmic, as in some religious painting. But it seems that it is inherent in feeling, as in thought, that it involve limit and then show that the deep individual not only accepts, but affirms the limit to his best hopes. One can't abandon either the hope nor the limit. But the limit is not abdication, but a sense of the condition of functioning. Without that the hope itself flies off into the shapeless.

He generalizes his position most succinctly in another letter to Hoyt, one dated 4 January 1950 [1951]:

I have had to work too hard to discover the actual to give it up lightly either in aesthetics or in politics. I want no "contemptus mundi," no peace outside nature & going concerns. A man must endorse something besides his own problems, or must come to.[17]

Many literary theorists will nowadays impatiently dismiss this search for and affirmation of the actual, never mind taking seriously a character's accepting limits that anyone else can recognize. For such theorists and their followers among the critics minds can meet only by chance; all crossroad encounters are accidental; persons cannot see eye to eye: everything is subjective; everyone is limited by his or her point of view, locked in soundproof, impenetrable cells. Certainly we are fated to be limited by our outlook and our very language. But we can talk about it. These theorists themselves engage in discourse! They try to impart their "texts." At the same time, they would stand on a platform outside the universe and snipe at it.[18] Despite their pronouncements, though, their feet must remain firmly on the ground; they cannot soar beyond the actual. Indeed, their very denial of the actual becomes its affirmation.[19] Some of us when we were students in Miller's classes used to try to compress this underlying idea, an adumbration of the midworld, in quasi-epigrammatic form: "You can't phone the phone company." (If you grasped it at once, you were qualified to join the Millerian circle!) It is not that the theorists assert that you *can* phone the phone company; it is that they insist that there is no phone company even as they dial numbers and expect others to pick up the receiver to listen to messages that are not intended to be composed of mantras.

Miller has anticipated this question begging. In the beginning was the word, after all; any denial of the word requires the language it cannot deny. History, of which literature is a part, is the story of experience related from a point of view arising from experience, the story of the revelation, revision, and reaffirmation of purpose the narrative of which itself continues the process and enlarges our self-awareness.

Notes

1. See Walter Kaufmann, *Philosophic Classics, Volume 1: From Thales to Ockham*, 2d. ed. (Englewood Cliffs, N.J.: Prentice-Hall, 1968), p. iii; Cushing Strout, *The Progressive Revolt in American History: Carl Becker and Charles Beard* (New Haven: Yale University Press, 1958), p. vii; Cushing Strout, *The Veracious Imagination: Essays on American History, Literature, and Biography* (Middletown, Conn.: Wesleyan University Press, 1981), p. 387; George P. Brockway, *Economics: What Went Wrong and Why and Some Things to Do about It* (New York: Harper, 1985), p. x; Robert H. Elias, *Theodore Dreiser: Apostle of Nature* (New York: Knopf, 1949), p. xii; Robert H. Elias, *"Entangling Alliances with None": An Essay on the Individual in the American Twenties* (New York: Norton, 1973), p. xv.

2. J. W. Miller, "The Paradox of Cause," *The Journal of Philosophy* 32 (1935): 171; reprinted with minimum editorial revisions in *The Paradox of Cause and Other Essays* (New York: Norton, 1978).

3. J. W. Miller, *The Philosophy of History with Reflections and Aphorisms* (New York: Norton, 1981), pp. 32–36. The text of this chapter is one that some of Miller's interested students— in particular, a handful of us who had graduated in 1936—began discussing many years ago, when, as was usual, one of us would receive a letter or essay written in longhand and then make a typescript to share with the others. This elucidation of purpose in history is one of the documents we circulated in the late thirties or early forties.

4. John William Ward, *The Special Program in American Civilization at Princeton* (Princeton, N.J., 1957), pp. [13–14]. In this booklet Ward explains that the program's introductory course, "Individualism in American Life," was designed to explore "what assumptions made belief in the free individual possible."

5. Miller defines dialectical opposition in *The Midworld of Symbols and Functioning Objects* (New York: Norton, 1982), pp. 185–86; he discusses freedom in a democratic society in chapter 7 of *Paradox of Cause*, pp. 97–105.

6. Charles Francis Adams, Jr. and Henry Adams, *Chapters of Erie* (Ithaca: Cornell University Press, 1956), p. 12.

7. Arthur M. Schlesinger, Jr., *The Age of Jackson* (Boston: Little, 1945), p. 369n.

8. Herbert Croly, *The Promise of American Life* (New York: Macmillan, 1909), p. 56.

9. Robert H. Wiebe, *The Search for Order, 1877–1920* (New York: Hill, 1967), pp. 11ff.

10. Michael Paul Rogin, *Ronald Reagan, the Movie, and Other Episodes in Political Demonology* (Berkeley: University of California Press, 1987), pp. 7–8.

11. *Columbia Literary History of the United States*, Emory Elliott et al., eds. (New York: Columbia University Press, 1988), p. xxi.

12. Daniel J. Boorstin, *The Americans*. 3 vols. (New York: Random House, 1958–73). The volumes are subtitled *The Colonial Experience* (1958), *The National Experience* (1965), and *The Democratic Experience* (1973).

13. Robert H. Elias, "History: Experience and the Soul of Time," *The American Scholar* 43 (1974): 308–18.

14. 14 June 1973. All letters from Miller to me are now in the Miller Archives, Williams College.

15. Denton J. Snider's *The State, Specially the American State, Psychologically Treated* (St. Louis, Mo.: Sigma, 1902), *The American Ten-Years' War, 1855–1865* (St. Louis, Mo.: Sigma, 1906), and *Abraham Lincoln. An Interpretation* (St. Louis, Mo.: Sigma, 1908) are his major contributions to the study of American history.

16. Daniel J. Boorstin, *The Discoverers* (New York: Random House, 1983), pp. xv–xvi.

17. Photocopies of the letters to Hoyt quoted in this article, along with some other letters in the correspondence, are in the Miller Archives; the originals of all the letters from Miller to Hoyt are at present in Hoyt's possession but will eventually be added to the collection.

18. Miller was fond of quoting Professor Asa H. Morton, a retired member of the Williams College faculty, who had said on an occasion I know nothing about: "You can't stand on a platform outside the universe and snipe at it."

19. Miller regards this idea as fundamental: "Stories of genesis are their own warrant. They have no prop, no crutch. Any supposed prop is itself a derivative and resultant of the process that it pretends to warrant. This process I call the *actual*" (*Midworld*, p. 7).

When the Truth Is in the Telling

Cushing Strout

Cornell University

IT is one of the inevitable consequences of our taking a historical view of the world that we include within it not only ourselves but the story of our coming to see it that way. For me the catalytic agent in that process was my teacher in philosophy, J. W. Miller of Williams College. The English philosopher R. G. Collingwood wrote in *An Autobiography:* "The chief business of twentieth-century philosophy is to reckon with twentieth-century history." He meant that we were on the threshold of an age in which history would be "as important for the world as natural science had been between 1600 and 1900." Only the philosopher who concentrated on the problems of historical inquiry and knowledge could help "lay the foundations of the future."[1] It was then 1939, the eve of the Second World War. In the following year, at Buenos Aires, José Ortega y Gasset would lecture on "Historical Reason" and announce: "The hour of the historical sciences is at hand. Pure reason . . . must be replaced by narrative reason. *Today* man is as he is because *yesterday* he was something else. Therefore, to understand what he is today we have only to relate what he was *yesterday*. . . . This narrative reason is 'historical reason.'"[2] Miller was quite abreast, in his own way, of this turn in philosophy, but I only began to feel its force after the war under the influence of his teaching.

As an infantryman in Europe I kept a notebook in order to keep alive the intellectual life that had been stimulated by being a student at Williams. My notes, however, show that my strongest intellectual interest during the war years was in Søren Kierkegaard's Christian existentialism. His anguished individualism with its focus on anxiety, dread, and despair was surely pertinent to my sense of life in the infantry, though fortunately his protestant intensity was qualified for me by G. K. Chesterton's more robust and humorous catholicism, which I had first encountered in my father's library. In my notebook for April 1945, written in Germany near the border of Czechoslovakia, as the war approached its end, I wrote that I had come to see that fascism had its philosophical rationale in the historicism of Hegel and

Gentile. I had been reading a book that defended the Natural Law theory of the Declaration of Independence against an historicism that "denying to the individual any significance apart from his membership in a group" undermines "the foundation of individual moral responsibility and makes impossible the world-wide sharing of an ideal of brotherhood." The author saw Vico as the origin of this form of historical relativism, its reactionary possibilities being made evident by "the ease with which it was woven into Fascist and Nazi ideology," and he accused both Vico and Benedetto Croce, who celebrated Vico's anti-intellectualism for being able to take myths seriously, of dangerous confusion in supposing that the study of myth should "be coloured by a positive attitude of appreciation."[3]

Eights months later, however, while recovering from pneumonia in Tilton General Hospital at Fort Dix, I had much time to read and bought a copy of Croce's *History as the Story of Liberty*. I discovered with excitement that historicism could be integrated with political and philosophical liberalism. (Croce was an enemy of the fascist regime; he survived only because his eminence beyond Italy's borders made it opportune for Mussolini to tolerate him.) I was impressed with Croce's reply to Kierkegaard's point that life could not be known in time because no moment of calm could be found in which to judge it. If such a moment could be found, I paraphased Croce in my notebook, "both the need and the ability to understand history would disappear."

I had not caught up fully yet with the time Collingwood and Ortega had enunciated, and the issues between Kierkegaard and Croce remained unresolved in my mind. But I find in my notebook an undated (probably 1945, when I was on a rest and recuperation furlough) reference to a conversation with Professor Miller, who provoked me to ask why there was no humor without bitterness in Kierkegaard and why there was no human realm of the undebatable for him. When I returned to Williams in my junior year, I intended to try and resolve my questions by doing an honors thesis on Kierkegaard. But Professor Miller, for whatever reasons, was not hospitable to the idea. (I wrote instead on American literature, following up Auden's remark in *New Year Letter* about its being "a literature of lonely people.") In retrospect, I think Miller not only believed that Kierkegaard had no place in the history of philosophy (in contrast to the history of religion), but he also recognized in the melancholy Dane a neurotic despair and wanted to steer me away from it. In any event, I took Miller's courses on American philosophy and the philosophy of history, as well as one, which he had launched, on the philosophy of the state, then being taught by his close colleague, Lawrence Beals. My experience of Miller's and Beals's humanistic secularity of thought decisively weaned me from Kierkegaard and prepared me for reading (outside of class) congenial historicists, certain thinkers who had not appeared on the syllabus: Croce, Collingwood, and Ortega.

Miller's role in my reorientation was fundamental and long-lasting. It is also hard to identify precisely because his teaching was more like Emerson's essays than it was like traditional philosophical argument. He was brilliantly aphoristic and epigrammatic, thinking out loud in a meditative and spontaneous way, sometimes obscurely and oracularly. Unlike Emerson, however, Miller had a strong feeling for institutions in general and for American ones in particular, as well as for liberal and democratic politics, freed of their contemporary materialistic, rationalistic, or sentimentally populistic tendencies. One kept at trying to understand him better by taking courses, which might all have been subtitled, as students used to say, Miller 7–8. I frequently pursued him down Spring Street after class and up to Grace Court and into his study where, sitting in a Morris chair, he would generously continue the meditation and discussion to my great profit. "Philosophy has no office hours," he used to say, and it was certainly a full-time activity for him, everything of interest going on in domestic politics, international affairs, and literary life (or in the College) providing him with apt examples and anecdotes. If you mentioned Freud's pleasure principle, he might say "it's always tea-time in the libido"; and I remember how quickly he responded when I mentioned Arthur Koestler's *The Yogi and the Commissar*: "That's a significant title, because neither the yogi nor the commissar represents personal responsibility; both are beyond criticism." He was Emerson's idea incarnate of the scholar as Man Thinking, and though his thought was nurtured by the tradition of German idealism, he was ultimately an American original, like Charles Ives, with a profound but critical attachment to his country and its history.

Miller's devotion to teaching and to his locality (having no car, his going even to nearby North Adams or Pittsfield was an unusual event) was remarkable, but it ran the risk of stranding him in a tidepool as the philosophical tides passed him by. For this reason I want to emphasize in his thought a theme that, though it does not take up much space in his recently published writings, vitally connects Miller's ideas with an important ongoing current in philosophical, historical, literary, and psychological thinking: the narrative quality of our experience and of our nonscientific knowledge. "What is at stake in the bearing of time on our identities is not only the materials of history books," as he put it. "It is rather all of the humanities and, indeed, all modes of learning in which there is nothing to be known apart from the telling."[4] This concern for what is implied in telling is now active in literary criticism, historical theory, and revisionist psychoanalysis because all three areas are deeply engaged with storytelling as fundamental to their inquiries.[5]

Miller was more interested in developing his own voluntaristic category of history than in annotating its ancestors, but in a letter, written to me on 4 July 1953, speaking of his stepping down from the chairmanship of philosophy, he made this observation about the early history of the idea of history:

> It is curious that the sense of history should have occurred first in Italy and Germany, two countries without much shape or force at that time. Perhaps the sense of things past needs more evident monuments to arouse it than we or the British possess, a past that is truly gone, irrecoverable and so capable of contemplation. Collingwood dug around for Roman remains, and tells in his autobiography how that affected his conception of knowledge and inquiry. . . . Perhaps Vico, in Naples, with Rome and Greece around him, felt the presence of a past that was not a mistake, but a life, while the truths of his own time reflected the implications of deeds, not the passivity of the intellect. Our voluntarism came from psychology, his came from history.

Vico, for Miller, was the "man who turned the corner away from the empiricism of 'fact' to that of the act. It is appalling to realize," he confessed, "that in 1922 when I got my degree I had not heard of him, although the Scienza Nuova appeared in 1725." There was some progress: "But things have moved. Some Heidegger is being translated. He is very hard to read in German, but I think he sees the role of the act and of the artifact. He unites historicism with existentialism." Miller rounded off his reflections with this prophecy: "Well, I think that this matter will be cleared up in the next twenty-five years." He responded to my query about whether he would use his retirement for writing (as I hoped he would) by saying: "One should start earlier in life, and with a more fluent command of language than I possess. Probably, too, with a different temperament. Besides, I do not find that I have any ideas not already published. Williams can give illusions of originality merely because many topics have been neglected here."

He spoke of clearing up Vico's legacy in twenty-five years;

exactly thirty years after Miller's letter, an anthology of articles from a vanguard intellectual journal included one by Sir Isaiah Berlin, tracing the significant distinction between knowing in the sciences and knowing in the humanities to the thought of Vico, who had first seen history "as a form of self knowledge incapable of ever becoming fully organized" and so had initiated a cleavage that "started a great debate of which the end is not in sight."[6] Miller's modesty about originality needs to be counterbalanced by taking account of a crucial fact: his own philosophy united historicism with existentialism in an original voluntaristic way that was highly appropriate to his teaching of American students at a time (when I encountered him) of much weight in our history. Moreover, in contrast to Heidegger's, Miller's thought and action were never contaminated by complicity with fascism and anti-Semitism.

Miller's reference to "voluntarism" in his letter indicates his own characteristic idiom in the philosophy of history. It focused on the pertinence of the category of history to action, limitation, freedom, destiny, responsibility, and finitude (one of his favorite terms). His reflections on history had an existential flavor, as in Lincoln's great formulation: "We cannot escape history." Like Lincoln, Miller was intellectually engaged with a time of crisis. The word *kairos* had been used to describe "a moment of fulfilled time" in reference to the intellectual ferment and excitement of Union Seminary in the 1930s "when Reinhold Niebuhr was in his prime, and Paul Tillich had just come."[7] We students heard Miller debate with both of these men in the 1940s, when his own views were very much in *kairos* because of their appropriateness to the historical time of our involvement with Europe in the war against fascism and later with Europe's rebuilding under the aegis of the Marshall Plan and NATO after the war. It was a time of risky and consequential deeds on a large scale, and it resonated with Miller's theme that commitment to "the relatively static" provided the occasion and the possibility for the dynamic developments of history, as it did for Lincoln (who was as much of a hero for Miller as he was for Niebuhr) with his revisionary dedication to the Declaration of Independence and the Constitution in the slavery crisis.

Miller's emphasis on "finite actuality," in contrast to the more infinite-oriented and cosmic philosophical idealism of the past, seemed profoundly relevant to the historical moment in which we came to participate, whether we wanted to or not, in the dangerous role of soldiers. Miller himself recognized that his version of idealism "exerts considerable appeal for young men, especially to those who have interposed their bodies and their wills between their country and its enemies."[8] A major consequence of his existential idiom, Hebraic rather than Greek, in Matthew Arnold's terms, was that it gave to written history and its problems much less attention than contemporary philosophers have given them. In the forties it was important for Miller to establish the category of history as a necessary one before he could do anything else with it; and the powerful influences of scientific rationalism, supernatural religion, and behavioristic psychology—all ahistoric in their orientation, like the political utopia of the world state, which was popular on college campuses—gave him much polemical work to do. Miller anticipated our current concerns, however, when he wrote: "A reader tends to accept as fact what the story needs for the telling. It is the story that empowers the reader to accept the facts. It gives him also the means of doubting. The writer himself furnishes those means" (*PH*, p. 125).[9]

It is necessary to insist, as he would later put it, that "the way of telling stories must also be made of nothing but experience."[10] This condition stands as a permanent barrier against the reductionist tendency to explain history in terms of entities that are not themselves generated by and in history, whether they be derived from concepts of God, nature, or psychology. "History writing that is not the imaginative reconstruction of past on its own terms, indeed the very discovery of such terms," as he incisively noted, "leaves the past as a mystery or else reduces it to the ahistoricity of scientific nature, to psychological atomism or theological incomprehension" (*PH*, pp. 186–87). An unreductive way of explaining history would have some affinity to myths because "whether Diana or English yeomen shoot arrows, the telling is indistinguishable in the common assumption of a local, a present, an active power" (*PH*, p. 151). From this point of view "it does not matter that Brutus may have misconstrued the motives of Caesar. Perhaps Caesar was more kind, or Brutus less disinterested, than Plutarch's story suggests. In any case the story is one of deeds done, and of what particular persons felt it necessary to do in a specific situation" (*PH*, p. 170).

It was the threat of psychological reductionism that for a time disrupted our correspondence in the late 1960s. Earlier, I had written about William James's complaint that his own philosophy was like "an unfinished arch, built only upon one side," and I had suggested that a philosophy of history might have finished his arch.[11] Miller's response was complimentary but also supplementary by way of elaborating his point that James tended to see our temporality as a mere matter of fact instead of as "a *factum*, as Vico speaks, something done, inseparable from doing, not an observation, not a truth, but an actuality."[12] What created loud static in our communication was my later use of Erik Erikson's concept of the identity crisis in working out the biographical and intellectual development of James's philosophy.[13] I had first read Ralph Barton Perry's two-volume work on James's letters during my hospitalization at the end of the war, and my return to that wealth of evidence some twenty years later took place during an extensive period that was highlighted by many valuable discussions with a friend and psychiatrist, Dr. Howard Feinstein. (He went on to write the highly regarded psychoanalytically informed biography, *Becoming William James.*)

My findings led Miller in two letters of 1968 to assert that "there is no point to an extended reply" if I viewed philosophy "as explained by non-philosophical events, or derived from some other discourse" than its own self-defining one.[14] His reply, nevertheless, was already extended to twenty-seven handwritten pages! Moreover, I had been careful in my treatment of James not to depend on Freudian theories of libidinal energy or of the oedipal explanation of neurosis. I did tell a story showing how in detail "a disturbed father did seek justification in his eldest son and that the disturbed son did to his cost and to his benefit 'overidentify' with him" (*VI*, p. 234). I did reject Collingwood's denigration of biography as unhistorical on the ground that since it is bracketed by birth and death, it is "a framework not of thought but of natural process."[15] James's "morbid traits" (as Perry called them) had meaning in the light of his family constellation and his career. The problem was to place his symptoms in the category not of causation but of development, to see them in relation to the circumstances of his life, his aspirations, and his conflicts. Collingwood himself insisted that the inner and outer in personality were not "mutually exclusive" because human individuality "consists not of separateness from environment but of the power to absorb environment into itself."[16]

I was careful also, because of my argument with Bill Miller, to point out that I had not made irrelevant the confronting of James with philosophical questions, nor had I settled anything about the truth or error of James's philosophy (*VI*, p. 231). Even so, Miller was adamant that no psychological question could be raised about philosophy without withering it, because its order is self-defining, as is history itself. Moreover, he did not think James's "brand of 'lostness'" was "of the simon-pure sort." People are attracted to

James's "capacity for sympathy," but "there is a lostness which is not met with sympathy. That is the genuine brand. It has a higher price and few will pay it." Was this a rare hint of a personal history? He concluded this somewhat enigmatic observation by saying that he "rejoiced in having escaped the futilities of pedagogy and the insincerities or contempt of the members of a learned profession."[17]

I was dismayed at this rupture and also by the tone of estrangement that went beyond our correspondence. In the early 1970s I wrote again on other issues, and we had broad agreement on the need to defend free speech on the campus when it was threatened or even suppressed, as it recurrently was, by some demonstrators, who had no understanding or respect for the open forum. In the spring of 1974 I paid a visit to him, while visiting my second son, who was a student at Williams, and in its wake I revived our correspondence on Erikson by indicating what it was about Miller's own thought that had led me to be receptive to this history-minded psychoanalyst in particular. Miller's response was much more amiable; even though his point was the same, I found it more understandable this time: " 'Explaining' experience always turned out to be parasitic on some state of affairs not within experience, a nameless mystery . . . On the other side, experience made absolute and exclusive forfeited any state of affairs which could give rise to it, criticize it, judge it, control its direction or modify any form to which it made claim. The 'Stream of Consciousness' had no banks and could have none."[18] The point was to find controlling categories in finite thought itself, but then these necessary ideas could not be explained without destroying their necessity. "The real is the order which permits theories," he had written before I knew him, "but it is not itself a theory nor derived from theory."[19]

Whatever the merits of this revisionary Kantianism as metaphysics (I am not qualified to judge), my interest as a historian in philosophy has always been in its bearing on inquiry in history, biography, and literature. From this point of view Miller spoke most directly to my concerns when he wrote that some historians' talk about hidden economic motives "never really tells what anybody did, but only what was brought about." The alternative would not be to look for "other and better or truer motives. That would not change the picture in principle." The point instead would be to look for "what events or statements determined an act," not as a form of "hidden motives and controls" but as "a *reaction* to a specific situation." Miller's argument depends on seeing that historical action does not operate "in terms of what men antecedently are. It operates in the disclosure of what they are in those reactions that serve to focus major energies" (*PH*, pp. 190–91).

My own version of this kind of historical explaining highlights the role of narrative because the logic of a historical situation is that of drama in which the "connective tissue" has "a dialectical form: a person or group takes a position and performs an action because of and in relation to the position or action of another person or group." So I wrote in 1960, adding that "this kind of historical action is understood in the same way as a novel's plot is understood, though the former must be faithful to given evidence and the latter to aesthetic standards" (*VI*, p. 39). It is in this sense that I understand Miller's point about the humanities as the place where the truth is in the telling. Paul Veyne, a contemporary French historian, has made a similar point: "Explaining, for a historian, means to show the unfolding of the plot, to make it understood."[20] Thus "causes" for a historian as "explanations" are not laws but summaries of a story.

That summarizing function is what Erikson's concept of the identity crisis did for me in my understanding of William James's relation to his father's ideas and his aspirations for his son. True, the terms of the account and its theme are mine, not his, but they both could *in principle* have been made clear to him as a story about his struggle to find his career, to become an agent in history.[21] The risk in this procedure is what happens in "psycho-history" when, as Frederick A. Olafson has justly remarked, the effect is "to shut the agent up within his own internal economy of feeling-states; and it is a real question in what sense the resultant analysis could count as 'historical' at all." Olafson envisages a solution in finding "a psychological vocabulary for describing an agent's intention" that "in effect incorporates many of the norms governing the social situation within which that agent lives and works." Then we would move away from "the picture of two sets of reasons—one operative and the other specious—for one action and toward a conception of these two sets of reasons as interpreting one another."[22] That is precisely what I think Erikson's vocabulary made possible for my construction of a narrative about James's career.

Novelists must face similar problems in telling stories in which actions and characters reveal each other. I have been particularly interested in novels which interact profoundly with some actual historical situation, thus creating a limited amount of common territory, a "border country" shared by historians and novelists. I moved into these concerns after the end of my relationship with Bill Miller. We never had really raised these issues. I have a postcard from him, however, sent from Florence on 9 February 1954, on the rare occasion of his excursion to Europe. It is a photograph of Donatello's Saint George. "What is the relation between art and history?" he asked, adding: "Wish we could talk." I am still asking myself that question, and I would echo his wish, anticipating the novelty and force of his ruminations, if the finitude he so respected and so richly made the center of his reflections had not made it impossible.

Miller did not live to participate in the contemporary debate over narrative form, and I can only speculate how he might have responded to it. I am confident, however, that he would have agreed with Louis Mink's subtle distinction between historical understanding and understanding history—as if it were merely a past "that we can understand as we do the present, through sociology or economics or whatever." If irony is a favored historical mode (as it is for both Niebuhr and C. Vann Woodward, for example), it is because thinking historically is being alert to how the process of becoming brings about results that are unforeseen by its agents. Such an ordering is retrospective, as Mink points out. The agents of becoming could not have understood the process any more than we can just by putting ourselves imaginatively into their situation.[23]

But if the order of the told depends upon the teller's perspective, how do we tell the novelist from the historian? Miller once suggested to me, when I was a student, that one difference between narrative history and narrative fiction should be a matter of focus. If Lincoln were the subject of a novel, for example, he should be seen not as trying to save the nation, as he would be seen in a history, but rather as trying to save his soul. The point is congruent with Olafson's argument that historiography cannot usually follow the novel in making an individual the story's center, nor can it give historical agents the kind of recognition scenes that are appropriate to tragic heroes.[24] Historians, like novelists, have to construct plots, but their focuses cannot be transfered from one medium to another, even though both kinds of writers have to evoke as well as describe, relate, and explain.

Some philosophers of narrative have been interested in it not only as an escape from the tyranny of the causal category but also from determinism. Miller, as a philosopher of freedom and responsibility, would surely have been of their company. In this light

I think he might also have found congenial a recent trend in American historiography, the study of slavery and working-class culture. Revisionist Marxists like Herbert Gutman and Eugene Genovese have replaced the conventional leftist category of victimization with an emphasis instead upon what the oppressed have done on their own intiatives, in spite of their hardships, to build a life of their own making. Miller was never a Marxist or a populist, but he respected the selves of ordinary people as much as he challenged the theoretical determinism that dominated our academic culture. In his day the specter was abroad among Marxists, behaviorists, and Freudians. Today the specter instead haunts the French poststructuralists, who fascinate so many literary theorists, with their denial of human agency in general and individual responsibility in particular.

Miller's theme of freedom as self-limitation is, in its antiutopianism, also profoundly alien to the limitless horizons so fondly cherished in much American rhetoric, whether of the Left or the Right. In this respect his life matched his thought: one wife, one college, one town. Kierkegaard was fond of citing the Socratic prayer that the inner man and the outer man would be one. That was the integrity of Miller's reclusive life.

Notes

1. R. G. Collingwood, *An Autobiography* (Oxford: Oxford University Press, 1939), p. 79.

2. José Ortega y Gasset, *Historical Reason*, trans. Philip W. Silver (New York: Norton, 1986), p. 118.

3. Laurence Stapleton, *Justice and World Society* (Chapel Hill: University of North Carolina Press, 1944), pp. 6, 37, 46.

4. J. W. Miller, *The Philosophy of History with Reflections and Aphorisms* (New York: Norton, 1981), p. 179. Hereafter, *PH*, with page references cited in the text.

5. The philosophers whom I have found to be most pertinent to reflections on historical narrative are William Dray, W. B. Gallie, Louis Mink, Maurice Mandelbaum, Frederick A. Olafson, and David Carr. Olafson and Paul Ricoeur have dealt with both historical and literary narrating. The historians I have paid most attention to on the narrative theme are J. H. Hexter, Paul Veyne, and Hayden White, particularly the first two. Georg Lukács and John Lukacs have focused on the historical novel. The revisionist psychoanalysts concerned with narrative theory are Donald Spence and Roy Schafer.

6. Isaiah Berlin, "The Divorce between the Sciences and the Humanities," *The Salmagundi Reader*, ed. Robert and Peggy Boyers (Bloomington: Indiana University Press, 1983), pp. 214–15.

7. Harold R. Landon, ed., *Reinhold Niebuhr: A Prophetic Voice of Our Time* (Greenwich, Conn.: Seabury Press, 1962), p. 11.

8. J. W. Miller, *The Paradox of Cause and Other Essays* (New York: Norton, 1978), p. 87.

9. See also Louis O. Mink, "History and Narrative" (1974), who notes that "the appro-

priateness of any factual description is controlled by the narrative order from which it is abstracted." Quoted in Brian Fay, Eugene O. Golob, and Richard T. Vann, eds., *Historical Understanding* (Ithaca: Cornell University Press, 1987), p. 24.

10. J. W. Miller, *In Defense of the Psychological* (New York: Norton, 1983), p. 9.

11. Cushing Strout, "The Unfinished Arch: William James and the Idea of History," *The Veracious Imagination: Essays on American History, Literature, and Biography* (Middletown, Conn.: Wesleyan University Press, 1981), pp. 44–56.

12. Letter to CS, 12 January 1962.

13. See my "William James and the Twice-born Sick Soul" and "Ego Psychology and the Historian," *The Veracious Imagination,* pp. 199–222; 223–44. Hereafter, *VI,* with page references cited in the text.

14. Letter to CS, 23 July 1968.

15. R. G. Collingwood, *The Idea of History* (Oxford: Oxford University Press, 1946), p. 304.

16. Ibid., p. 162.

17. Letter to CS, 23 July 1968. The other chastising letter is dated simply July 1968.

18. Letter to CS, 23 April 1974.

19. J. W. Miller, "For Idealism," *The Journal of Speculative Philosophy* 1, no. 4 (1987):266. I am indebted to Professor Joseph Fell for bringing this article to my attention.

20. Paul Veyne, *Writing History: Essay on Epistemology,* trans. Mina Moore-Rinvolucri (Middletown, Conn.: Wesleyan University Press, 1971), p. 88.

21. On adapting an existential-psychoanalytic investigation to Collingwood's idealistic model of mind, see Louis O. Mink, "Collingwood's Dialectic of History," in Fay et al., eds., *Historical Understanding,* p. 262.

22. Frederick A. Olafson. *The Dialectic of Action: A Philosophical Interpretation of History and the Humanities* (Chicago: University of Chicago Press, 1979), pp. 284–85, n.31.

23. Mink, "Phenomenology and Historical Understanding," in Fay et al., eds., *Historical Understanding,* pp. 108, 116.

24. Olafson, *Dialectic of Action,* pp. 79–81.

IV
Bibliography

A Miller Bibliography
with a Brief Description of
The Williams College Miller Archives

Henry W. Johnstone, Jr.

DISSERTATION

"The Definition of the Thing." Ph.D. diss., Harvard University, 1922. Printed in *The Definition of the Thing with Some Notes on Language,* 7–168. New York: W. W. Norton, 1980.

BOOKS BY MILLER

The Paradox of Cause and Other Essays. New York: W. W. Norton, 1978.

The Definition of the Thing with Some Notes on Language. New York: W. W. Norton, 1980.

The Philosophy of History with Reflections and Aphorisms. New York: W. W. Norton, 1981.

The Midworld of Symbols and Functioning Objects. New York: W. W. Norton, 1982.

In Defense of the Psychological. New York: W. W. Norton, 1983.

OTHER PHILOSOPHICAL WRITINGS BY MILLER

"The Paradox of Cause." *The Journal of Philosophy* 32 (March 1935): 169–75. Reprinted with revisions in *The Paradox of Cause and Other Essays,* 11–18.

"Accidents Will Happen." *The Journal of Philosophy* 34 (March 1937): 121–31. Reprinted in *The Paradox of Cause and Other Essays,* 42–55.

"Motives for Existentialism." *Comment* (Williamstown, Mass.) 1 (Spring 1948): 3–7.

Review of Walter A. Kaufmann, *Nietzsche: Philosopher, Psychologist, Antichrist. Williams Alumni Review* 43 (May 1951): 149–50.

"Afterword: The Ahistoric and the Historic." In José Ortega y Gasset, *History as a System and Other Essays toward a Philosophy of History,* 237–69. New York: W. W. Norton, 1961.

"Discovering the Limits of 'Right to Dissent'." *Evening Sentinel* (Ansonia, Conn.), 3 September 1970, 4.

"History and Case History." *The American Scholar* 49 (Spring 1980): 241–43.

"For Idealism." *The Journal of Speculative Philosophy* 1 (Fall 1987): 260–69.

"The Owl." *Transactions of the Charles S. Peirce Society* 24 (Summer 1988): 399–407.

"On Choosing Right and Wrong." *Studies in Idealistic Philosophy.* Forthcoming.

REVIEWS OF INDIVIDUAL BOOKS BY MILLER

The Paradox of Cause and Other Essays (1978)

Abelson, Raziel. *New Leader,* 15 January 1979, 18–19.

Anderson, James F. *The Review of Metaphysics* 33 (September 1979): 189–90.

Choice 16 (June 1979): 544.

Hunt, Thomas C. *Library Journal* 103 (November 1978): 2244.

Kirkus Reviews 46 (15 August 1978): 933.

Radest, Howard B. *Bibliographie de la philosophie* 28, no. 4 (1981): 203.

Singer, Peter. *New York Review of Books,* 22 March 1979, 30–32.

The Definition of the Thing with Some Notes on Language (1980)

Armour, Leslie. *Library Journal* 105 (November 1980): 2330.

Baillie, Hal. *Best Sellers* 40 (December 1980): 340.

Bates, Stanley. *Ethics* 92 (October 1981): 181–82.

Choice 18 (January 1981): 673.

Kirkus Reviews 48 (15 August 1980): 1141–42.

The Philosophy of History with Reflections and Aphorisms (1981)

Choice 19 (December 1981): 516–17.
Dray, William H. *American Historical Review* 87 (June 1982): 745.
Kerlin, Michael J. *Thomist* 49 (January 1985): 132–34.
Keymer, David K. *Library Journal* 106 (August 1981): 1546.
Kirkus Reviews 49 (1 July 1981): 856.
Tyman, Stephen. *History and Theory* 23, no. 1 (1984): 132–40.

The Midworld of Symbols and Functioning Objects (1982)

Armour, Leslie. *Library Journal* 107 (May 1982): 892.
Chronicle of Higher Education, 5 May 1982, 22.

In Defense of the Psychological (1983)

Choice 21 (October 1983): 354–55.
Kirkus Reviews 51 (15 March 1983): 358.
O'Brien, Robert C. *Library Journal* 108 (May 1983): 1005.

OTHER WRITINGS ABOUT MILLER, INCLUDING COMPOSITE REVIEWS OR CRITICAL STUDIES OF HIS BOOKS

Brockway, George P. "John William Miller." *The American Scholar* 49 (Spring 1980): 236–40. Reprinted in Joseph Epstein, ed., *Masters: Portraits of Great Teachers,* 155–64. New York: Basic Books, 1981.
Colapietro, Vincent. Review of Miller's five books. *The Journal of Speculative Philosophy* 1 (Summer 1987): 239–56.
———. "Reason, Conflict, and Violence: John William Miller's Conception of Philosophy." *Transactions of the Charles S. Peirce Society* 25 (Spring 1989): 175–90.
Corrington, Robert S. "John William Miller and the Ontology of the Midworld." *Transactions of the Charles S. Peirce Society* 22 (Spring 1986): 165–88.
———. "Introduction to 'For Idealism'." *The Journal of Speculative Philosophy* 1 (Fall 1987): 257–59.
———. "John William Miller's 'The Owl'." *Transactions of the*

Charles S. Peirce Society 24 (Summer 1988): 395–98.

Fell, Joseph P. "An American Original." Critical Study of Miller's
   five books. *The American Scholar* 53 (Winter 1983–84): 123–30.

Friend, Theodore. Review of Miller's five books. *Yale Review* 73
   (Spring 1984): 446–51.

Furtwangler, Albert. "Stones, Histories, and Cases." *Dalhousie Review* 67, nos. 2–3 (1988): 328–34.

Gahringer, Robert E. "John William Miller" (memorial minute).
   Proceedings and Addresses of the American Philosophical Association
   52 (March 1979): 518–19.

THE MILLER ARCHIVES AT WILLIAMS COLLEGE

The Miller Archives comprise a collection of Miller's work housed
in boxes containing numbered folders that include the following
material:

Papers before the 1970s

Essays	Boxes 1–3
Essay Drafts	Boxes 4–8
Notes	Boxes 8–17
Letter Drafts	Boxes 18–19
Diaries	Box 19
Mailed Letters	Boxes 19–22
Letters to Miller	Box 22
Students' Notes and Papers	Box 22

Acknowledgments

I wish to extend special thanks to the following for their indispensable help: George P. Brockway; Vincent Colapietro; Joseph P. Fell; Sylvia B. Kennick, Archivist, Williamsiana Collection, Williams College; Noelene P. Martin, Pattee Library, The Pennsylvania State University; Eugene R. Miller; and Rohit Sanghi, Research Assistant, Bucknell University.